Movies, Radio, and Television: 250 Anecdotes

David Bruce

Published by David Bruce, 2024.

While every precaution has been taken in the preparation of this book, the publisher assumes no responsibility for errors or omissions, or for damages resulting from the use of the information contained herein.

MOVIES, RADIO, AND TELEVISION: 250 ANECDOTES

First edition. December 24, 2024.

Copyright © 2024 David Bruce.

ISBN: 979-8230603030

Written by David Bruce.

Table of Contents

Dedication

Dedicated to Amateur and Professional Creative People

Rise above.

Theater director Tyrone Guthrie advised his actors and crew to do this. The advice means to rise above whatever forces are working against you. All of us have personal problems. No one's life is perfect. Sometimes, life seems to conspire against us. Rise above all that, and produce the best work you can.

Astonish me.

Dance impresario Sergei Diaghilev advised his choreographers to do this. The advice means what it says. Do such good work that the person who commissioned the work — and of course the audience — is astonished. (Tyrone Guthrie also used this phrase.)

Do it now.

As a young man, choreographer George Balanchine nearly died and so he believed in living his life day by day and not holding anything back. He would tell his dancers, "Why are you stingy with yourselves? Why are you holding back? What are you saving for — for another time? There are no other times. There is only now. Right now." Throughout his career, including before he became world renowned, he worked with what he had, not complaining about wanting a bigger budget or better dancers. One of the pieces of advice Mr. Balanchine gave over and over was this: "Do it now."

Go out and get one.

Ruth St. Denis once taught Martha Graham an important lesson when Ms. Graham was just starting to dance. Ms. St. Denis told Ms. Graham, "Show me your dance." Ms. Graham replied, "I don't have one," and Ms. St. Denis advised, "Well, dear, go out and *get* one." (Everyone needs an art to practice. Your art need not be dance. Perhaps your art can be writing autobiographical essays. Of course, you may practice more than one art.)

Assign yourself.

The parents of Marian Wright Edelman were serious about education. Each school night, she and her siblings were expected to sit down and do their homework. Whenever one of the children said that the teacher had not assigned any homework, her father used to say, "Well, assign yourself." Ms. Edelman once made out a list of "Twenty-Five Lessons for Life," based on the values she had learned from her parents. Lesson 3 was, "Assign yourself. Don't wait around to be told what to do." In 1973, she founded the Children's Defense Fund, which attempts to get federal legislation passed to help children.

Challenge yourself.

Joss Whelon created the TV series *Buffy the Vampire Slayer*, which is noted for its clever dialogue. Day after day, people told Joss that they watched the series because of its dialogue, so he decided to challenge himself by writing an episode in which the characters could not talk. The episode, titled "Hush," is excellent and was nominated for an Emmy.

Practice an art.

The father of choreographer Bella Lewitzky taught her the importance of having an art to practice. He worked at an ordinary job, but when he came home, he painted. Ms. Lewitzky says, "He taught me that it didn't make a d*mn bit of difference what you did for a living, as long as you had something that rewarded your life." He also didn't feel that it was necessary to have an audience for his art because the act of creation was rewarding in itself. Bella and her sister used to steal their father's paintings — because if they didn't, he would paint another work of art on top of the one he had already created.

Do it yourself.

Early in their career, the Ramones played in London on July 4, 1976. Some cool kids who called themselves The Clash hung around during a sound check before the concert and talked to the members of the band, mentioning that they played music but weren't good enough to play in public. Johnny Ramone told them, "Are you kidding? I hope you're coming tonight. We're lousy. We can't play. If you wait until you

can play, you'll be too old to get up there. We stink, really. But it's great."
(This is a great example of punk rock's do-it-yourself attitude. You don't
need a lot of fancy equipment to play music. Just teach yourself a few
chords, get up on stage, and rock. Similarly, if you want to write, you
don't need a lot of fancy equipment. If you have a computer, great, but
all you really need is some paper and a pencil or pen.)

Be there.

After retiring from her career in dance, Balanchine dancer Barbara
Milberg became a very good student — and eventually a Ph.D. (and
professor). In dance, she had learned that when the curtain went up,
she had better be there, and so she never handed in a paper late.

Get it right.

A man — who didn't dance — visited the dance class of Margaret
Craske. At the end of her class, he said goodbye and jokingly executed
a *port de bras*. Quickly, Ms. Craske reached out and corrected the
position of the visitor's hand. As you would expect, in her dance classes,
she tells her students over and over, "Get it right!"

***

Educate Yourself
Read Like A Wolf Eats
Be Excellent to Each Other
Books Then, Books Now, Books Forever

Chapter 1: From Academy Awards to Censorship

Academy Awards

• On 23 March 2003, Michael Moore won an Oscar for Best Documentary: *Bowling for Columbine*. This was during the time that President George W. Bush was leading the United States into war with Iraq because of a false claim that Iraq had weapons of mass destruction. In his speech on worldwide television, Mr. Moore said, in part, "We live in a time where we have a man sending us to war for fictitious reasons. Whether it's the fiction of duct tape or the fiction of orange alerts: we are against this war, Mr. Bush. Shame on you, Mr. Bush. Shame on you! And anytime you've got the Pope and the Dixie Chicks against you, your time is up! Thank you very much." Lots of people at the event booed—very loudly—and a stagehand yelled at him as he left the stage. (The stagehand later apologized after discovering that Mr. Moore was right.) People threatened Mr. Moore, and he hired ex-Navy Seals as bodyguards. But good things happened, also. After the Oscars ceremony, Mr. Moore and his wife went to the Governors Ball. Sherry Lansing, the head of Paramount Pictures, walked up to him. Mr. Moore was afraid that he was going to be shouted at by the very powerful Ms. Lansing, but she kissed him on the cheek and said, "Thank you. It hurts now. Someday you'll be proved right. I'm so proud of you." Then she hugged him in public to show the public her support of Mr. Moore. Robert Friedman, another very powerful person at Paramount, hugged Mr. Moore's wife and shook Mr. Moore's hand.[1]

• Quite a number of famous actors have kept their Oscars in the bathroom: Sean Connery, Tim Robbins, Susan Sarandon, Elizabeth Taylor, Charlize Theron, Emma Thompson, Rachel Weisz, and Kate Winslet. Jodie Foster used to, but she removed them after their bottoms started corroding. Ms. Winslet has a good reason for keeping her Oscar in the bathroom: "Because basically everybody wants to touch it, everybody wants to hold it. So I figured if I put it [in the bathroom], then people can avoid the whole, 'Where's your Oscar?' thing … [guests] can sneakily have a little [hold] and put it back down again." On the other hand, Timothy Hutton keeps his in the refrigerator. He and his sister were going to have a party, and Mr. Hutton says that "she thought it would be funny to put the Oscar in the refrigerator when people would go grab a beer or something." Now, many years later, "It's still there." Jimmy Stewart made good use of the Oscar he won for his role in *The Philadelphia Story*. He sent it to his father, where for years it was on display in the family hardware store in Indiana, PA.[2]

Activism

• Don't mess with 75-year-old Mona Shaw of Virginia. The elderly woman ordered services from her cable company, Comcast. The installers were supposed to come by on a certain day. Sure enough, they showed up—two days late. They were supposed to complete the installation. They did not. Mrs. Shaw and her husband went to the Comcast office to speak to the manager. They waited for one hour. Then they waited for another hour. Then they were informed that the Comcast manager had left for the day and would not return. Mrs. Shaw left, but she returned—with a hammer. She attacked a Comcast computer with the hammer, yelling, "Have I got your attention now?" Police restrained her with handcuffs and took her away. Consumers everywhere thought, "You go, girl." They also thought, "Let's play word association. What do I think of when I think of Comcast? Well, obviously, I think of bad service."[3]

Acting and Actors

• In 2007, Noomi Rapace read for the part of Lisbeth Salander, the punk computer expert in Stieg Larsson's *Millennium* trilogy, in the Swedish film version of *The Girl With the Dragon Tattoo*. She got the role, and played Lisbeth in three Swedish movies. The movies made her a star, and suddenly she was able to work with pretty much anyone she wanted to work with. Like many people, she had some misconceptions about Los Angeles, as her manager, Shelley Browning, who represents many foreign citizens who work in Hollywood and who has long known Ms. Rapace's Swedish agent, discovered. Ms. Rapace said, "I thought L.A. was more about celebrities and red carpets and glossy big lips and big tits. I said to Shelley when we met, 'I don't want to go to Hollywood. That's not for me. I want to do real movies.' And then she said, 'But who do you actually like?' I started to mention people, and she said, 'Those people actually live in L.A.'" Of course, many misconceptions about actors exist, and they are held even by people who should know better. One misconception was revealed when Ms. Rapace began to meet people in Los Angeles. Ms. Browning said, "It was quite funny, when you work in a business where artists are chameleons, because they kept calling me and saying, 'She's nothing like Lisbeth Salander.' And I said, 'What did you expect? She was going to come in on a Harley, with a leather jacket and piercings?' And they said, 'No, but like, nothing! She's beautiful, she's funny, she's feminine.' It wasn't like one or two people called me, it was like everybody called me." Another misconception could be about actors' glamorous lives: Actors don't sweat. But one of the people Ms. Rapace wanted to work with was director Ridley Scott. Ms. Rapace got to meet Mr. Ripley. She said, "I never get nervous, but I thought I was going to pass out. I had on this blue Helmut Lang dress, and when I started to sweat, you could really see it." By the way, Mariah Larsson, a research fellow in cinema studies at Stockholm University, pointed out, "If you just read Swedish newspapers, you would think there are three big stars in Hollywood: Stellan Skarsgard, Noomi Rapace, and Alexander Skarsgard."[4]

• Jamie Kaler starred in the TBS comedy *My Boys*, on which he played Mike Callahan. In his life, he has shown a lot of persistence. After resigning his commission in the United States Navy, he wanted a job in a certain bar on the beach at San Diego. The bar did not have any job openings, but he returned to seek employment at the bar 27 days in a row, and the bar hired him. He started taking acting classes, and he started acting in commercials, including a commercial for Sea World: "All I did was watch Shamu jump, and that was it. But I made a boatload of money off it, and I immediately thought, 'This is going to be the easiest profession ever.' But I didn't get another job for a year." He also learned early to live life. In San Diego, he roomed with John David Lenz, a dedicated actor who died young: "I'd wake up on a Saturday morning having bartended and been out drinking, and he'd be playing *Henry V* and quoting the movie with Laurence Olivier. And he ended up dying. He got shot [...] walking to his car, a random shooting by a 15-year-old girl. So I had to come home to the apartment and pack up his stuff, sell his car and had to help his parents take all his stuff out of the house. And then we all went back to Kansas for the funeral. I think after that I was, 'Man, I've got to get busy living. It's all going to end.'" He kept acting, picking up more and more roles, but he never officially quit his night-time bartending job: "Finally the owner called and said, 'Dude, you haven't worked in nine months, do you still work here?' I said, 'No, I guess I don't.'"[5]

• Tom Baker was the actor who played the Doctor Who with the absurdly long scarf — the result of a woman who was given lots of wool to knit and who was so excited to be working on Doctor Who's costume that she did not stop knitting until she ran out of wool. The budget for *Doctor Who* was small, with the result that sometimes scenes had to be filmed again because the scenery shook. Mr. Baker said in a *Guardian* (UK) interview, "As an actor, walking through a door naturally is an art, and someone once told me that they'd never seen anyone do it as well as me. I didn't like to say that it was because the BBC sets shook, and the doors had to be closed gently." In one *Doctor Who* adventure, "The Deadly Assassin," the good doctor nearly drowned. This was an episode that Mr. Baker really wanted to see when it was broadcast — no video or DVD recorders existed back then. He remembers, "I was on a signing tour of the country at the time, and I knocked on the door of a house in Preston, just as a father was settling down to watch it with his two five-year-old sons. He said nothing and just beckoned me inside. I crept into the room and sat quietly in a chair and, as my face came up on screen, you could see the stupefaction on the kids' faces as they noticed me. How could one person be in two places at once? It was just ecstasy. But the whole process of making *Doctor Who* was a joy."[6]

• Jennifer Love Hewitt acquired her middle name because when her mother, Pat, was studying speech pathology in college, her best friend was a beautiful woman named Love. She acquired her first name because when she was born, her older brother, Todd, thought that she might want a more normal name because "Love" was a weird name. His parents allowed Todd to choose his sister's first name, and because he liked a girl named Jennifer in the neighborhood, he named her "Jennifer." Of course, Love (as she is called) became a famous actress, an occupation that led to some interesting experiences. For example, in 1994 she had her first on-screen kiss in the TV movie *The Bryds of Paradise*, which was filmed in Hawaii. To get the kiss right, she and her co-star had to work at it—they practiced kissing in some bushes until they could kiss well enough for the filming of the scene. Love says, "I had never kissed anyone before in my whole life, and I was scared half to death." Later, when she was a cast member of the TV series *Party of Five*, her character frequently kissed the character played by Scott Wolf, who played a teenager but was in real life 10 years older than the character he played. Love said at the time, "Wow, I'm the luckiest teenager alive—kissing an older man everyday *and* getting paid for it!" [7]

• In the finale of the 1992 film *Sneakers*, the hero played by Robert Redford is being chased by several bad guys. Stephen Tobolowsky, who played bad-guy character Werner Brandes, tells an anecdote about director Phil Alden Robinson letting the bad-guy actors know in which order they should chase Mr. Redford. Mr. Robinson said, "Let's do it this way. [Sir] Ben [Kingsley], you're the Academy Award winner, we'll start with you. Then, Tim [Besfield], the Emmy winner, you'll be next. Do we have a Tony winner? Anyway, Stephen, you'll be last." Mr. Tobolowsky also tells what he calls a "Hollywood Zen story": "We shot on location around Los Angeles and at Universal. The studio has a going concern of little buses that regularly drive through the back lot area with tourists from all over the world wielding disposable cameras. The tour guide has a set patter, 'On your right is the shark from *Jaws*. On your left is Columbo's automobile.' While one of the buses was nearing our stage, we were called to the set. The tour bus had to stop while Robert Redford and James Earl Jones crossed in front of it. No one noticed. The guide just kept up with, 'On our right is the bicycle from *E.T.*' People were snapping away at the bicycle and were completely oblivious that two of the most famous actors in the world were a few feet away from them."[8]

• In 1972, film director Michael Winner made the film *Death Wish*, starring Charles Bronson. In it, the "hero" is a man whose family is attacked, and who then becomes a vigilante. Mr. Winner and Mr. Bronson had made a movie titled *The Stone Killer* together, and Mr. Bronson asked Mr. Winner, "What should we do next?" Mr. Winner said, "Charlie, I've had a script for some time called *Death Wish*. ... It's about a man whose wife and daughter are mugged, and he goes out and kills muggers." Mr. Bronson said, "I'd like to do that." Mr. Winner asked, "The film?" Mr. Bronson showed that he was the perfect person to star in the movie by saying, "No, I'd like to kill muggers." By the way, when Mr. Winner directed Orson Welles in the movie *I'll Never Forget What's 'isname*, Mr. Welles complained, "Michael, you're shooting me from below. That will make me look fat." Mr. Winner comments, "Orson would have looked fat if you'd shot him from a helicopter."[9]

• Mary Tyler Moore missed out on the chance to play one of Danny Thomas' daughters in his TV series because Mr. Thomas believed that no one would believe that someone with a nose like hers could be a daughter of his, but fortunately she was later chosen to play Laura Petrie—the story is that Danny Thomas, who financed the pilot of the *The Dick Van Dyke Show*, was handed a list of actresses and was asked, "Can you think of any more?" The word "more" caused Mr. Thomas to think of Mary Tyler Moore and so she auditioned for—and got—the part. Throughout the first year of *The Dick Van Dyke Show*, Danny Thomas made a point of writing "Boo!" and "Hiss!" on Mary Tyler Moore's checks because he had heard of an old Chinese belief that the gods are kind to young people whom elders dislike. By writing "Boo!" and "Hiss!" on her checks, Mr. Thomas made sure that the gods liked Ms. Moore.[10]

• Lena Headey, who starred as the title character in Fox-TV's *Terminator: The Sarah Connor Chronicles*, says that she has had numerous encounters with ghosts throughout her life. In one case, she had just bought a house and as she was lying on the bed it started shaking. Other events occurred. For example, she put a rabbit sculpture on a shelf and the sculpture fell off—nine times. Her boyfriend was skeptical about the ghost, saying, "Oh, rubbish!" But when the two discovered that a chest of drawers had been pushed against a door so that no one could open it, she asked him, "Now do you believe?" Ms. Headey thought of the ghost as a little boy, and she made peace with him: "I said, 'You can be here but don't scare me,' and it stopped."[11]

• When cartoon producer Leon Schlessinger asked Mel Blanc to create the voice of Porky Pig, Mr. Blanc asked for time to do some research. Mr. Schlessinger was surprised by the request, but agreed. Mr. Blanc drove out to a pig farm to study the pigs and listen to them grunt. However, he decided to turn the series of grunts into a stutter. He also decided to have Porky Pig attempt to say several words before saying a different word. He then drove to see Mr. Schlessinger and auditioned the voice: "Porky would say good-bye like this: 'Bye-b—, uh-bye-b—, so lo—, uh-so-lon, auf Wiede—, auf Wiede—, Toodle-loo.'" Mr. Schlessinger loved the voice and gave Mr. Blanc the job, but he also told him, "Go home and take a bath, will you?"[12]

• Amy Ryan admires director Sidney Lumet, working with him on the TV series *100 Centre Street* and the movie *Before the Devil Knows You're Dead*. According to Ms. Ryan, "The great gift from Sidney, among many, is he really feels actors can do no wrong." As evidence, she cites the example of her appearing on his TV series *100 Centre Street* in one episode, and only three episodes later being asked to appear again in the series, but playing a different character. She said in answer to Mr. Lumet's request, "Sidney, yes, of course, thanks, but how am I going to pull this off?" He replied, "You're a good enough actor—you'll figure it out." According to Ms. Ryan, "If that man can give the OK to that, you think, 'Oh wow, maybe I can do anything.'"[13]

• Actress/model June Wilkinson was not afraid of nudity, and she appeared in *Playboy* a number of times. In interviews, she gave different reporters different measurements. If a reporter acted like a jerk, she told him something ridiculous, such as her bust was 44 inches. If a reporter acted like a gentleman, she gave him her real bust size: 40 inches. Ms. Wilkinson (40-23-36) once guest-starred on the TV series Batman, starring Adam West and Burt Ward. While she was being made up, Mr. West and Mr. Ward walked in and started talking about her and her physique. Eventually, Ms. Wilkinson gave herself away by giggling.[14]

• Jennifer Love Hewitt had a tough time in junior high school. The other kids were jealous because she was missing school to work as an actress, and sometimes they would throw Coke on her. When she was a somewhat older actress acting in *Party of Five*, two of her junior-high tormenters saw her at a 7-Eleven near her house and said to her, "We just love *Party of Five*. Would you mind signing something?" She replied, "You know what? Sorry, I can't. I have to go. Really nice to see you. Bye-bye." She adds, "I wanted to say something really mean, but why go to their level?"[15]

• The second movie that veteran actor Saul Rubinek ever did was an independent movie titled *Death Ship*, although the cast referred to it as *Death Sh*t*. Mr. Rubinek remembers leaving the production trailer one day and seeing his fellow cast members immersed in water. This was shocking because of a production report that stated that no actors should ever be in the water because of really bad pollution. Mr. Rubinek says that "apparently nobody had told the actors. And that's when I began to understand something about the nature of independent movies."[16]

• In 2010, actress Cate Blanchett co-starred as Maid Marian in Ridley Scott's movie *Robin Hood*, a role in which she impressed her three sons because of a mishap. On the first day of shooting the movie, she was supposed to shoot a flaming arrow. However, she missed the target and instead hit a light—which exploded. Ms. Blanchett asks, "How many mums do stuff like that?" By the way, when she appeared on a postage stamp in the "Australian Legends of the Screen" series, she joked, "I'm going to be licked by millions of Australians, and I can't wait."[17]

• *The Dick Van Dyke Show* and *The Andy Griffith Show* were filmed close to each other. One day, Don Knotts, who played Deputy Barney Fife on *The Andy Griffith Show*, went to see the cast of *The Dick Van Dyke Show* rehearse. He asked the show's creator, Carl Reiner, what Mr. Van Dyke was like, explaining that he had never met him. Mr. Reiner replied, "You want to know how nice Dick Van Dyke is? I'll tell you. You're a nice guy, Don. He's nicer."[18]

• Andy Pryor, casting director for *Doctor Who*, sometimes receives in the mail unsolicited materials from actors. Sometimes, these are annoying. In an interview with the *Guardian*'s Laura Barnett, he said, "The worst is when you get a card with a teabag in it, and the card is filled with glitter — so that when you open it, it goes all over you. They say, 'We just wanted to get your attention.' It's like, 'Yes, you did. Now we've got to clean this sh[*]t up.'"[19]

• Stephen Spielberg was so impressed by Pete Postlethwaite's performance as the villainous William S. Holabird in the Spielberg-directed movie *Amistad* that he called Mr. Postlethwaite "the best actor in the world." Wittily, and modestly, Mr. Postlethwaite said that Mr. Spielberg must have been misquoted: What Mr. Spielberg most likely said was that Mr. Postlethwaite "*thinks* he is the best actor in the world."[20]

• Linda Thorson played Tara King in the British tongue-in-cheek TV series *The Avengers* alongside Patrick Macnee, who played John Steed. Just out of drama school, she had a hard time adjusting to the rigors of the series. She said, "I was too fat for karate, too breathless for the fight scenes, and too busty for the love bits. They had to pour my 39-inch bosom into 36-inch sweaters so Patrick Macnee could get near me."[21]

• Joe Franklin frequently had British actor Arthur Treacher on his talk show; however, Mr. Treacher had absolutely no problem walking off the show if he ever felt bored. He would simply tell Mr. Franklin, "Ooh, Joe, the old man's getting cranky now, the old man's getting grouchy, the old man's getting tired." Then he would get up and walk off.[22]

• Sissy Spacek won an Oscar for Best Actress after playing country singer Loretta Lynn in *Coal Miner's Daughter*. Afterward, big-breasted country singer Dolly Parton sent her this telegram: "Dear Sissy, I hope you make millions of dollars from *Coal Miner's Daughter* so that you can get a boob job and do the Dolly Parton story."[23]

• Mae West knew what she wanted. Seeing a tall, dark, handsome man on the Paramount movie lot, she knew that she wanted him as a co-star for her movie *She Done Him Wrong*. She did her own casting, and she said, "If he can talk, I'll take him." The tall, dark, handsome man was Cary Grant, who was still early in his film career.[24]

• Sissy Spacek won an Oscar for Best Actress after playing country singer Loretta Lynn in *Coal Miner's Daughter*. Afterward, big-breasted country singer Dolly Parton sent her this telegram: "Dear Sissy, I hope you make millions of dollars from *Coal Miner's Daughter* so that you can get a boob job and do the Dolly Parton story."[25]

• Kevin Spacey acted with Jack Lemmon in a few movies. He remembers that immediately before each take Mr. Lemmon would quietly say to himself, "It's magic time." Magic time resulted in two Oscar wins for Mr. Lemmon. This ritual is something that he did each time he acted, including in the theater and on TV.[26]

• Robert Mitchum played tough guys in the movies, and he was a tough guy. Often, idiots would try to fight him. Once, he was sitting quietly in a bar when someone came up to him and threw a punch to his cheekbone. Mr. Mitchum simply said to the man, "I hope that isn't your best punch." The patrons in the bar applauded.[27]

• After retiring as an actor, Western star Randolph Scott wanted to join the Los Angeles Country Club—which did not accept actors. According to legend, when he was told that he couldn't join because he was an actor, Mr. Randolph replied, "Oh, really? Have you seen my work?"[28]

• Victor Mature was not known as a great actor, but he never let that bother him. A director once asked him for more expression in a retake of a scene, and Mr. Mature replied, "I have two expressions: full face and profile. Which do you want?"[29]

Advertising

• Roger Corman made many, many low-budget movies, and he was a master at making a profit from them. One of his apprentices was Allan Arkush, who directed *Rock 'n' Roll High School* with the Ramones for him. Mr. Arkush put together many trailers for Mr. Corman's movies. He knew that Mr. Corman's audiences liked action, and so he inserted an "exploding helicopter shot" into many of the trailers even when the movie did not have an exploding helicopter.

Another of his apprentices was James Cameron, director of *The Terminator*, *Titanic*, and *Avatar*. Mr. Corman saw *The Terminator* and asked Mr. Cameron how he was able to have the movie look so good. Mr. Cameron replied, "It was easy. We did the same thing we did when we worked for you. We just got to do it with more money."[30]

• In the early part of his career, actor Jim Backus worked as an announcer in radio. One of his sponsors was the P.O.C. Beer Company. Once, Mr. Backus did an on-location interview with a chef who talked only about wine. Wanting to get his sponsor into the interview, he said to the chef, "And I'll bet to a lot of diners you recommend that they drink P.O.C. beer with their meal." The chef glared at Mr. Backus and said, "Beer is for pigs!" Then he added, "Beer is slop. It causes gas! It dulls the taste buds! Maybe if you are outdoors, a sip of Heineken or a swallow of Muenchner is permissible, but that garbage P.O.C.! Never! Phooey!" Mr. Backus was fired.[31]

• Glenhall Taylor and Frank Gage once created and performed a comedy radio show called "Frankie and Johnny." Most of their "sponsors" were fictional, but they did have one real sponsor in Ptomaine Tommy's, a greasy spoon restaurant. Mr. Taylor and Mr. Gage used to make fun of Ptomaine Tommy's on the air, saying things like "Don't make fun of Tommy's coffee—you may be old and weak yourself someday" or "Don't order the hash—Tommy can't remember what's in it." Eventually, Ptomaine Tommy stopped sponsoring the show—the advertising had given the restaurant too many customers. [32]

• In the 1970s, Dannon used a group of centenarian Georgians to advertise its yogurt, implicitly suggesting that the yogurt was what made the Georgians so long-lived. Getting the Georgians to agree to do the TV commercials was easy—the producers simply gave them USAmerican-made blue jeans and ballpoint pens. There was one problem, however. To keep on friendly terms with the Georgians, each

USAmerican had to drink a bottle of vodka a day. (Perhaps the vodka is the real reason the Georgians are so long lived.)[33]

Advice

• Walt Disney, host of TV's *The Wonderful World of Disney*, knew what the public wanted, and he was very good at giving it what it wanted. This applied to more than movies, television, and theme parks. Walt's pilot, Kelvin Bailey, remembers when he and Mr. Disney ate breakfast in a hotel restaurant by the waterway in San Antonio, Texas. Walt did the good deed of talking to the restaurant's manager and giving him some advice: "I've been looking at this room here. It's a very nice room, but may I make a couple of suggestions? You need to engender an image of hospitality, and if you were to change the design here, make this archway round instead of square, add a coat of blue instead of green, put a chandelier here ...." Walt spoke for 30 minutes, and some staff members of the restaurant took notes. One year later, Kelvin visited the same hotel restaurant. All of the changes that Walt had mentioned had been made, and the manager told him that since the changes had been made, the restaurant had been a gold mine. (By the way, Walt followed his own advice. He once visited Disneyland and saw that it needed a new coat of paint. He told the engineer in charge of maintenance, "I want this place painted." The engineer replied, "OK, Walt. We'll do it over the weekend." Walt replied, "No, I want it painted tonight and finished by morning." All was done exactly as he wished.) Walt did other good deeds as well. While on the job, comic-strip artist Floyd Gottfredson received a call that his wife was ill and going to a hospital. He told Walt that he would be gone for the day. Walt asked, "You got a car?" He did not. Walt said, "How will you get out there? Here, take my car." And he gave Floyd his car keys.[34]

Animals

• Benny Washam, a former resident of Possum Foot Bridge, Arkansas, told cartoon director Chuck Jones that a certain story of the Johnson Brothers—both oversized and under-brained—who lived in nearby Cotton Mouth Farm was true. The Johnson brothers had a profession: pig-rustling. They rustled a pig, loading her into the back of their pickup, but soon they heard on the radio that the police were on the lookout for anyone who was hauling a pig. To avoid unnecessary trouble, they dressed the pig in a shirt and pants that belonged to a Johnson grandmother who weighed approximately the same as the pig: about 500 pounds. They then put the pig in the seat between them. Sure enough, two state troopers stopped them and asked them who they were. They identified themselves as Johnsons, and then gave their first names: Frobe, Newt, and Oink. The state troopers let them go, and one state trooper said to the other, "Have you ever in your born life seen anybody as ugly as that Oink Johnson?"[35]

• Philip Baker Hall starred in the 2007 movie *Duck*, and yes, his co-star was a duck. Well, actually several ducks. Adult ducks look very much alike, and different ducks were used for different scenes. Mr. Hall explains, "The director determined that some ducks were better for certain moods than others. So if we needed a duck that was nervous or sort of grouchy, that would be, like, #25…and if we needed a duck that listened well quietly and seemed to be absorbing dialogue, that was Duck #34." So what is like to have a duck as a co-star? Mr. Hall says, "Well, what it means is that you have to learn 100 pages of dialogue yourself!"[36]

• Celebrity interviewer and talk-show host Joe Franklin once had a singing dog on his program. Unfortunately, before the program started, the dog made a mess on the floor. Mr. Franklin asked the dog's owner, "What's that all about?" The owner responded, "He's clearing his throat."[37]

Art

• The television show *Melrose Place*, which was set in a Los Angeles, California, apartment complex, featured much work by up-and-coming artists. Conceptual artist Mel Chin once said, "Everyone criticizes television, but nobody tries to intervene to give it the meaning it lacks." Therefore, Mr. Chin founded the GALA Committee to try to give television some culture. Mr. Chin approached *Melrose Place* set decorator Deborah Siegel with the idea of placing avant-garde works of art in the show's episodes, and she immediately agreed. The GALA Committee and Ms. Siegel collected works of art from around the country and worked them into the show, giving viewers a dose of culture. Some of the art was subversive. For example, Courtney Thorne-Smith's character was featured in a couple of episodes struggling with an unplanned pregnancy. She snuggled in a quilt in those episodes: The quilt was decorated with the molecular structure of the abortion drug RU-486.[38]

Alcohol

• A number of people who work in movies enjoy a drink or two or several. When Charlie Chaplin was working on a certain movie, he had a camera man who would tell him when it was getting close to quitting time, "Charlie, the light's better in Oldfield's." Oldfield's was a tavern that belonged to Barney Oldfield.[39]

Audiences

• In a theater, Charles Bukowski saw *Tales of Ordinary Madness*, a movie in which Ben Gazzara played him. Mr. Bukowski was drinking, and he kept yelling criticism during the movie. In one scene, Mr. Gazzara kept typing while a beautiful prostitute lay down on his bed. Seeing that, Mr. Bukowski yelled, "If that were me, I would have stopped typing long ago!" Seeing a scene set in a flophouse, Mr. Bukowski yelled, "I've never seen a flophouse as empty and clean as that one." Some of the movie patrons did not care for the running criticism, and one yelled at him to shut up. Mr. Bukowski yelled back, "Hey, I'm the guy they made the movie about. I can say anything I want to. You shut up."[40]

Auditions

• Bill Cosby knew that he wanted the Huxtable family on *The Cosby Show* to be like real life in many ways. Malcolm-Jamal Warner played the role of Theo, the Huxtables' son. He says, "When I auditioned, I played a real smart-alecky kid, huffin' and puffin.'" Mr. Cosby asked him, "Do you really talk to your father like that?" Malcolm-Jamal replied, "No." Mr. Cosby said, "Then we won't see that in the show." Malcolm-Jamal then auditioned in a more realistic manner and got the part.[41]

Awards

• Mike Nichols and Elaine May satirized television, among other targets. At an Emmy Awards show, Ms. May, acting as host, praised everyone who had won for excellence, then said, "But what about others in the industry? Seriously, there are men in the industry who go on, year in and year out, quietly and unassumingly producing garbage." She then announced an award for the Most Total Mediocrity in the Industry. Accepting the award was Mr. Nichols, who said, "This is the proudest moment of my life. I'd like to say briefly how I did it. Firstly, no matter what suggestion the sponsors make, I take them. Last but most important, I have tried to offend no one anywhere on earth. In ten years of production, we have received not one letter of complaint." [42]

• The high-quality TV sitcom *Taxi* won awards even when it had low ratings. After it was canceled, it still won Emmys. When Judd Hirsch, who played Alex Rieger, picked up an Emmy for Best Award in a Comedy Series, he asked, "Don't they know we've been cancelled?" [43]

B Movies

• It is possible to make a movie for the fun of it while not expecting — and perhaps not wanting — a lot of people to see it. For example, 1980s pop princess Debbie Gibson made the television B movie *Mega Shark vs. Giant Octopus* for the Syfy channel after her agent brought the acting opportunity to her attention. She says, "I figured die-hard science fiction fans would see it, and that's it. Fun, kitschy — and under the radar." Fun, yes. Kitschy, yes. Under the radar, no. Actually, millions of people saw the movie. When her agent called Ms. Gibson to tell her how many people had seen the movie, he began the conversation by saying, "Please don't fire me."[44]

Baseball

• Joe Garagiola once asked Chuck Connors, the television star of *The Rifleman* and a major league baseball player at one time, which was tougher—baseball or television. Mr. Connors replied, "Baseball's tougher. The difference is in one word—retake. If they had retakes in baseball, I'd have wound up in the Hall of Fame."[45]

Bathrooms

• In June 2015, Henry Rollins finished filming a movie titled *The Last Heist*, directed by Mike Mendez, who likes lots of murder and blood in his films. Henry plays a "completely diabolical" character named Bernard and spends much of the movie covered in fake blood. One day, completely covered in fake blood, he was walking to the restroom. The movie was being filmed in an industrial area of Glendale, California, and a man driving a forklift saw him and deadpanned, "Rough day?" Mr. Rollins says that the blood dries quickly and becomes sticky: "I was, at times, a murderous candy apple dipped in dirt and debris. A fly actually got stuck in my hair and buzzed in frustration."[46]

Beauty

• When Oprah Winfrey was a young woman, she entered and won some important beauty contests—in 1972 she was crowned both Miss Black Nashville and Miss Black Tennessee. Nevertheless, she did not consider herself beautiful; instead of winning by virtue of beauty, she won through being articulate, intelligent, and interesting when asked questions by the judges and by coming in first in the talent part of the contest. Sometimes, the other, undeniably pretty contestants were upset when she won, and Ms. Winfrey told them, "Beats me, girls. I'm as shocked as you are."[47]

Birth

• British actress Prunella Scales, who played the wife of Basil Fawlty in *Fawlty Towers*, was married to Shakespearian actor Timothy West. Both did television and movies and so were used to doing retakes to get things right. When Prunella gave birth to their elder son, Sam, Tim was present. He looked at Sam and said, "Very good — no retakes." Prunella says that she "laughed so much that I had to have stitches."[48]

Cartoons

• Chuck Jones directed many cartoons that featured such stars as Bugs Bunny and Daffy Duck. Someone asked author Ray Bradbury at his 55th birthday party, "What do you want to be when you grow up?" Mr. Bradbury replied, "I want to be 14 years old like Chuck Jones." Of course, cartoon characters such as Bugs Bunny have a life and a reality of their own. Someone once introduced Mr. Jones to a six-year-old boy as the man who draws Bugs Bunny. The six-year-old boy corrected him—"He draws *pictures of* Bugs Bunny."[49]

Censorship

• The mother of playwright Frank McGuinness was a movie buff. How much of a movie buff? She risked excommunication from the Catholic Church in order to see *Duel in the Sun*, starring Jennifer Jones and Gregory Peck—a movie that the Bishop of Derry in 1946 had forbidden Catholics to see. His mother lived in Buncrana, Ireland, but she and a friend went to Derry to see the movie. They planned to leave before the lights came on at the end of the movie, but they enjoyed the movie so much that they stayed until the very end. His mother whispered to her friend, "It's all right. Nobody will know us." But when the lights came on, they looked around and saw all of their neighbors, who had also gone to Derry to see the forbidden movie.[50]

• *M*A*S*H* features physicians who frequently operate on wounded soldiers, so yes, the operating scenes do feature blood (but no open wounds). Occasionally, the TV network censors would ask the show not to spend so much time on scenes set in the operating room. One network censor even pointed out that he had seen the movie in the theater, and two women had walked out when an operating scene was shown. Gene Reynolds, producer of the TV sitcom, replied, "Fourteen million of them stayed!"[51]

Chapter 2: From Children to Emmys

Children

• When Bill Hanna of Hanna-Barbera cartoon fame was very young, his family had what he called a chicken house. Lots of glass was in the chicken house, and he got the idea of throwing a stone at a pane of glass. It broke and made a beautiful pattern of cracks. He and a sister, Lucille, had a good time cracking the other windows in the chicken house. Young Bill did not get spanked for doing this, but one time he did get spanked. After school, he had gone to a place that had donkeys and horses, and he had spent a lot of time there without letting his mother—who was understandably very worried—know where he was. At his mother's insistence, his father spanked him—sort of. Out of sight of his mother, his father removed his belt and said, "Bend over." Then he said, "I want you to cry loud enough so that your mother can hear so that she'll be convinced you're getting a real spanking." Actually, a chair received a lot more of the force of the belt than Bill's bottom did, and Bill was a good enough actor that his mother thought that he had actually been spanked. Bill was pretty creative even early in life. This is a poem that he wrote about his new sister, Evelyn: "I have a brand-new sister / I haven't held her yet / Each time I start to pick her up / Her diaper's wringing wet."[52]

• *Friends* co-star Jennifer Aniston was a very imaginative child. As a toddler, she created a world of imaginary Little People. One day, she started crying and told her father that he had stepped on several of them. He played along, picking the Little People up and straightening them out, and he told young Jennifer that perhaps she should put the Little People in the bathtub so that they wouldn't get stepped on. On another occasion, Jennifer was outside riding her tricycle when she suddenly screamed. Her mother came running because she was afraid that Jennifer had fallen off her tricycle, but Jennifer complained that the grass had been talking to her. John, Jennifer's brother, called her the "queen of make-believe." John was eight years older than Jennifer, and he had a tree house. Because Jennifer was allowed to enter the tree house, she had to guess the secret password. The password was always the name of a player on John's favorite football team: the Dallas Cowboys. Even when she was three years old, Jennifer was able to guess the password. As a teenager, Jennifer started to wear the SoHo fashion of all-black clothing. Her Greek grandmother, Yaya (the Aniston family name was originally Anistonapoulos), wondered why Jennifer was dressing like a widow.[53]

• For eight seasons, Chuck Norris starred in the TV series *Walker, Texas Ranger*. One day when Chuck's son Eric was 10 years old, Chuck drove him to school. As he always did, Eric kissed his dad goodbye. Another kid saw him, laughed, and asked, "Do you still kiss your dad?" Eric grabbed the other kid's shirt, pulled him close, and said, "Yeah. What of it?" The other kid stopped laughing and then said, "Oh, nothing." Chuck says, "I witnessed the incident and was so proud of my son that I could hardly contain myself." By the way, this is a Chuck Norris Fact: "When Superman goes to bed, he wears Chuck Norris pajamas." Here is another: "Faster than a speeding bullet, more powerful than a locomotive, able to leap tall buildings with a single bound ... yes, these are some of Chuck Norris' warm-up exercises."[54]

• As a kid, Matt Groening (famous for *The Simpsons* TV series and the *Life in Hell* series of cartoons) and his friends were mischievous. He and his friends sometimes sneaked into an old zoo that had closed so they could play in the empty animal cages. Matt even swam in the pool of water located in what used to be an enclosure for bears. In addition, he was mischievous at the new zoo, where he used to hide until he could hop on the zoo's miniature train and ride without paying. While the miniature train track was being built, Matt and his brothers pushed a train car to the top of a hill and then rode it on the tracks downhill. Unfortunately, the train was going so fast that it jumped the track and Matt and his brothers had to run away from the police.[55]

• Art Linkletter is famous in large part because of his funny question-and-answer sessions with children, but other celebrities have also interviewed children. One such celebrity is Ed McMahon, who is most famous for his many years as Johnny Carson's sidekick on *The Tonight Show*. He interviewed children on a TV morning show called *Strictly for the Girls*. He once asked, "When should a girl marry?" The answers included "If she ever kisses a boy," "Not until she's six years old, " and "I'm never gonna be married." He once asked a boy, "Do your mommy and daddy take care of you?" The boy replied, "Well, it's mostly my mother." Mr. McMahon then asked, "Does your daddy help?" The boy said, "Sometimes, but my mommy's mad at him because he pees in the bathtub."[56]

• On May 26, 2010, radio and TV personality Art Linkletter died. He was especially known for his interviews with children, an idea that occurred to him after talking to his young son, Jack, who told him why he did not want to return to kindergarten after his first day of school: "Because I can't read, I can't write, and they won't let me talk." Mr. Linkletter once asked a child, "What does your mommy do?" The child replied, "She does a little housework, then sits around all day reading the Racing Form." And when he asked another child what animal he would like to be, the child replied that he wanted to be an octopus so that he could grab bullies with his "testicles."[57]

• Broadcast journalist Connie Chung's family came from China, and she was the first member of her family to be born in the United States. Her sisters decided to give her a USAmerican name, so they pulled out a copy of the movie-star magazine *Photoplay* and decided to turn to a page at random and name her after whichever movie star was featured on that page. That movie star was Constance Moore. Even at age four, Connie knew that she wanted to interview people like the broadcast journalists she saw on TV. She even pretended that a metal tube from a vacuum cleaner was a microphone while she "interviewed" her friends.[58]

• TV's Katie Couric is perky. When she was very young, she used to memorize photos and names from an older sister's high-school yearbook, and at football games, she would do such things as go up to a student and say, "Hi! You're Barbara McLaughlin. I recognize you from the picture in my sister's yearbook!" As an adult, she wrote and edited a book in which she passed on advice from famous and successful friends: *The Best Advice I Ever Got: Lessons from Extraordinary Lives*. In the Introduction to the book, she quotes Oscar Wilde: "I always pass on good advice. It is the only thing to do with it. It is never of any use to oneself."[59]

• When cartoon director Chuck Jones had his sixth birthday, his parents got him a birthday cake. His mother handed him a knife and told him to cut as big a slice as he wanted to eat. Young Chuck gave her the knife back and said that he was going to eat *all* of the birthday cake—he had no desire to share any of it with anyone. The adult Mr. Jones drew on such experiences as this to develop the selfishness of Daffy Duck. (Chuck and Daffy define "selfish" as "honest but antisocial," and they define "unselfish" as "socially acceptable but often dishonest.")[60]

• Johnny Carson loved children, even when they said something—unintentionally—at his expense. He once had as guests on *The Tonight Show* two 2nd-grade girls who sold jokes for a penny each. Before he began buying jokes, he asked the two little girls if they had ever seen his late-night talk show. One little girl replied, "Yes, but I fell asleep." On another show was an eight-year-old child named Joey Lawrence. When Johnny asked Joey if he had ever seen his show, Joey replied, "Yes — one night when I was throwing up."[61]

• When Barbara Feldon, who played the role of Agent 99 on TV's *Get Smart*, was in the second grade, her mother realized that no one would be in the house one day when young Barbara came back from school. Therefore, her mother asked Pat, Barbara's sister, to write a number of math problems on a sheet of paper. Barbara came home, saw the math problems, and worked on them until someone came home. Because she was working on the math problems, she did not worry about being in the home alone.[62]

• A woman named Elaine Madsen used to write letters to movie critic Roger Ebert in the 1960s. She was married and lived on the Southwest Side of Chicago. In one letter, she asked Mr. Ebert if she should let her children see *The Night of the Living Dead*. He advised her not to, and she followed his advice. Years later, two of her children—Michael and Virginia—were famous actors. Michael confessed that he had snuck out and seen the movie when he was nine years old. He told his mother, "You were right. I shouldn't have seen it." [63]

• USAmerican movies are seen all over the world, and children watch them. Groucho Marx, host of the radio and TV quiz show *You Bet Your Life*, once visited Dornum, Germany, where his mother had been born. An eight-year-old boy asked, in German, where Groucho was from. Groucho replied, "Chicago," and because the boy had seen lots of Chicago gangster movies, he pretended that his hand was a pistol, pointed it at Groucho, and said, "Bang! Bang! Bang!"[64]

• The first movie that *Slate* movie reviewer Willa Paskin ever saw — she was three years old — was *The Muppets Take Manhattan*, which came out in 1984. Near the end of the movie, a car hit beloved character Kermit the Frog. Ms. Paskin remembers, "My mother looked over to see if I was okay, but I was gone, out of my seat, halfway up the aisle and heading for the door. I was not going to sit there and watch anything awful happen to Kermit the Frog."[65]

• Irish actor Jason O'Mara and USAmerican actress Paige Turco have a young son, and of course they wondered whether he would also become an actor. Mr. O'Mara said, "From the looks of it, my son's going to be an actor, too. He's very dramatic." As evidence, he said that at age five, his son was looking in the mirror and saying, "Daddy, daddy, this is my sad face." Of course, this makes his parents cry, "Oh, no! He's going to be an actor!"[66]

• Britney Spears knew what she wanted from a very early age. For one thing, she wanted to be one of the Mouseketeers on the *Mickey Mouse Club* TV show. She tried out for the show, but she was rejected because of her youth. Later, she tried out for the show again, and this time she was accepted. Exultant, the 11-year-old said, "It was all I'd really wanted since I was eight!"[67]

• During an interview with the child guests on his TV show, Art Linkletter told a little girl to imagine she had $10, then he asked her what she would buy. She answered, "I would buy my parents some pajamas, because they sleep together without any clothes on."[68]

Christmas

• Comedian Red Skelton sometimes did not give enough credit to his writers, although he did pay them well. On *The Tonight Show*, host Jack Parr asked him where he got his jokes. Red replied, "All my jokes are put in my head by the voice of God." His writers asked Red why he had not given them credit. Red replied, "You're just sore because I gave God top billing." The writers figured that if God was going to get top billing, He had better work for it, so they gave Red the script for his next show: fifty blank pages. They also gave him this note: "Dear Red: Please have God fill in the empty pages. Thanks. Your Writers." By the way, maybe God did deserve some credit for putting jokes into Red's head. Red once fell very ill and needed an operation. He was wheeled into the operating room, and the surgeons found this note written on a piece of tape on his chest: "DO NOT OPEN UNTIL CHRISTMAS." And when Red's movie *Half a Hero* turned to be very bad, Red complained, "They were afraid to show it at Grauman's Chinese Theater for fear the footprints would get up and walk away." [69]

• Charlie Lederer was a Hollywood scriptwriter with a knack for revenge. If someone did something to annoy him, Mr. Lederer would get him. One Christmas, producer David Selznick had fun opening his presents, keeping a huge present—one about 12 feet long—for last. Finally, he unwrapped that present. Inside was a long pole, with this note attached: "Mr. Selznick, this is the ten-foot pole I wouldn't touch you with. Charles Lederer."[70]

• In 1899, actor Humphrey Bogart was born on Christmas, and he wasn't happy about it, complaining, "Got gypped out of a proper birthday, g*dd*mnit." In 1946, comedian W.C. Fields died on Christmas—a holiday he always claimed to despise.[71]

Clothing

• Movie actress Marion Davies liked to have lots of female guests stay with her in the mansion of her lover, William Randolph Hearst. Ms. Davies had lots of fine clothing, and her female guests would get up early in the morning and raid her closets. Ms. Davies, who slept late, once said, "In this house, the first girl up is the best dressed." Mr. Hearst, of course, was fabulously rich and made many purchases of art and other desirable items. He once saw photographs of a set of Irish silver in an old art magazine, and he ordered a member of his staff to find out who owned the Irish silver so that he could buy it. She tried, but could not, so she hired a Private Investigator to find its owner. The PI sent her this telegram: "This item was purchased six years ago by W.R. Hearst of California." The set of Irish silver was still in a packing case in a warehouse full of valuable items.[72]

• Lucille Ball was the star of *I Love Lucy*, but co-star Vivian Vance was perhaps the funniest one off-screen. Tallulah Bankhead once guested on the show, and when Lucy said that she liked the sweater that Tallulah was wearing, Tallulah insisted on giving it to her, although Lucy pointed out that *I Love Lucy* was No. 1 in the ratings, and so she could afford to buy her own sweater. Vivian watched with interest as Tallulah insisted that Lucy take the sweater that she said she liked, and then Vivian said, "Tallulah, I love those pants." By the way, Vivian had to gain weight in order to appear on *I Love Lucy* because Lucy, a former glamorous model, wanted to be the prettiest one in the show. Lucy would call her up once a year and say, "Viv, dear, we start shooting in a couple of weeks. Start eating!"[73]

• Mabel Albertson played a lot of mothers in old sitcoms. She was Rob Petrie's mother in *The Dick Van Dyke Show*, Don Hollinger's mother in *That Girl*, and Darrin Stevens' mother in *Bewitched*. However, early in her career, she was a comedy writer, and whenever she went out on dates, she had a stock of ad-libs she would tell her gentlemen friends. For example, if her date admired her evening dress, she would say, "It's a biblical dress—low and behold."[74]

• Censors occasionally worried about *The Dick Van Dyke Show*. For example, a sponsor representative once told series creator Carl Reiner, "You've got to watch the undercupping." Mr. Reiner didn't know what he meant, so the representative explained that when Laura Petrie wears a tight dress, "Her behind is sculptured too well!" Mr. Reiner replied, "I'm not watching any undercupping—you watch it."[75]

• One of Mary Tyler Moore's breaks came when she was hired to play Sam, the receptionist on *Richard Diamond, Private Eye*. The only thing the TV viewer saw of Sam was her legs because her face was never shown on TV (to make her more mysterious). While playing the role of Sam, Ms. Moore sometimes wore hair curlers on the set![76]

• As everyone does who lives long enough, Marlene Dietrich aged. Her famous legs swelled because of circulation problems, so she designed boots tall enough to cover the swelling. Because the degree of swelling varied considerably, she had her boots manufactured in several different sizes so she could always find one pair that fit.[77]

• Tim Conway sometimes created outlandish suits for the times when he and Harvey Korman ate out together—or at home. Once, he made a suit with the same pattern as the wallpaper in his living room so that he could disappear by blending into the background.[78]

Comedians

• Johnny Carson, host of *The Tonight Show* for many years, was a quick-witted man who came up with his own jokes — and who delivered expertly the jokes his writers came up with. Joan Embrey of the San Diego Zoo often brought exotic animals on his show, and a marmoset once climbed onto Johnny and sat on Johnny's head. Johnny looked into the camera and said, "Tell me one other place in this whole world of seven billion people where a man is sitting with a marmoset on his head." A man once asked him, "What made you a star?" Johnny replied, "I started out in a gaseous state and then I cooled." Ed McMahon, Johnny's *Tonight Show* sidekick and friend, was often the good-natured recipient of Johnny's jokes about his supposed excessive intake of alcohol. Once, Johnny said, "Actually, Ed has good control of his drinking. He drinks only in places that have walls." Of course, funny things sometimes happened to him. Fairly early in his career, he and Mr. McMahon were sitting together in a restaurant when they noticed two elderly ladies looking at them and smiling. One elderly lady told the other, "You go." The other elderly lady replied, "No, you go." When they had settled who should go, one elderly lady approached their table. Mr. Carson and Mr. McMahon thought that she was going to ask them for autographs, but the elderly lady said, "If you're not using the cream, may we have it?"[79]

• Gilda Radner of *Saturday Night Live* fame was an original. She was ambitious, and she wanted to be on lots of sketches on the show, and she tried to figure out ways to make that happen. Once, the writers were working in the middle of the night, and they needed help from Gilda, so they called her. She told them, "I'm in bed!" But she also said that she would be right over. Soon, she arrived, wearing pajamas. Actually, she had been fully dressed when the writers called, but she put on pajamas so that the writers would feel sorry for her and write funny material for her. Once, Gilda liked a guy in Brazil and she thought that he liked her, too. He invited her to spend Christmas at his home, and she agreed, so she flew all the way to Brazil. When she got there, the man introduced him to his girlfriend. Gilda said, "How do you do? May I use your phone?" She called a cab and within three minutes was on her way to the airport to go back home to the United States.[80]

• When Joan Rivers appeared on *The Tonight Show* for the first time, she was nervous. In fact, she was so nervous that to bolster herself she wrote "Good luck" on one of her knees and "Break a leg" on her other knee. (Her dress covered the words.) She was a success, but she had reason to be nervous: She had auditioned for *The Tonight Show* a few times but had always been rejected. It is definitely a confidence buster to audition for a secretary who is eating a sandwich—and who then rejects you![81]

Crime

• As a very young man, actor Steve McQueen broke into homes and stole. According to Mr. McQueen, "I never made off with very much. I really took just what I needed to buy food." Later, he felt guilty about what he had done, and twenty years later his adventures in theft, he visited the homes to try to make amends. He says, "I'd knock on doors. People looked very surprised to see me standing there and I'd ask if they remembered someone breaking into the house. Some said they couldn't recall, or that they were broken into more than once, but some said they did remember. Then I'd say, 'I have a friend who did it and he asked me if I'd come and pay you back,' and I'd pay them and leave before they asked questions. That made me feel a little better."[82]

• Frederick Dey was the creator of Nick Carter, an internationally known hero of dime novels in the late 19th century and a radio series in the mid-20th century. People believed that Mr. Carter was real and even wrote letters to him. Once, Mr. Dey visited Paris, where he and a friend were surrounded by six hoodlums. Mr. Dey raised a fist in the air, shouted, "*Je suit* Nick Carter," and the hoodlums ran for their lives.[83]

• In September of 2007, Keifer Sutherland spent a couple of months in jail because of DUI (driving under the influence) charges. Afterward, he went on David Letterman's late-night show and talked about the time that he dropped his soap in the jail showers and decided not to pick it up, explaining, "It was at that point I decided that soap was overrated."[84]

• The car that belonged to TV's Mister Rogers was stolen. Fortunately, he had left some personal belongings, including a script of his TV show, in the car. A day later, the car was found in the exact spot from which it was stolen, with an apology note on the seat: "Sorry. We didn't know it was your car." (Is this an urban legend? Possibly, but it sounds plausible.)[85]

Critics

• When the movie *The Bourne Ultimatum* premiered in 2007, nearly all established movie critics rushed to praise it. For a while, the only negative review appearing on the Rotten Tomatoes website was written by *Washington Post* movie reviewer Stephen Hunter. Someone wrote movie critic Roger Ebert to ask if he felt that Mr. Hunter was embarrassed at being the only movie critic on Rotten Tomatoes to pan the movie, but Mr. Ebert wrote back, "I think it's a badge of honor for Stephen Hunter. When only one review disagrees, read it. I did, and understand his point, even if I disagree." Mr. Ebert did ask Mr. Hunter about being the only movie critic on Rotten Tomatoes panning the movie, and Mr. Hunter replied, "I'm far too shallow to have doubts." (Of course, a few other movie critics eventually wrote negative reviews of *The Bourne Ultimatum*, so Mr. Hunter was the first rather than the only movie critic on Rotten Tomatoes to pan the movie.)[86]

• Roger Ebert was the first critic to review a movie by Martin Scorsese: his student film titled *Who's That Knocking on My Door?* In his review, Mr. Ebert wrote, "In ten years, he'll be the American Fellini." Mr. Scorsese telephoned Mr. Ebert and asked him, "Geez, do you think it's gonna take that long?"[87]

Death

• When George Burns died at the age of 100 years and 49 days, he was encrypted in Forest Lawn with his longtime comedy partner and beloved wife, Gracie Allen. The inscription on the crypt said, "Gracie Allen and George Burns — Together Again." When Gracie was alive, the act was always Burns and Allen, but in death she got top billing.[88]

Directors

• Lots of famous movie directors have directed television programs, although doing so can be different from directing a movie. For example, Patty Jenkins, director of *Monster*, directed the pilot episode of the TV series *The Killing* and ordered many more takes than a television director, who often must work quickly, would order. David Madden, president of Fox Television Studios, said, "I'd watch her [Ms. Jenkins] go 12, 13, 14 takes. For a line producer, that's justifiable cause for a heart attack." In addition, when Antoine Fuqua, director of *Training Day*, directed a television pilot, he says, "I took the exact same approach as I would with a movie," meaning that he used many wide shots and crowd scenes rather than television-friendly close-ups. However, he had to learn to keep in mind that television has commercials: "They'd remind me about act breaks for commercials, and I'd go, 'What's an act break?'" When Martin Scorsese directed the pilot episode of *Boardwalk Empire*, his reputation as a big-time movie director was so intimidating that people stayed out of his way. Terence Winter, executive producer of *Boardwalk Empire*, said, "We were laughing because normally you're on the set and it's your show. [Instead, we] hung out at craft services." Mr. Winter did once want to make a suggestion. A 1920s gangster kept his hat on when he entered a room that was filled with women, and Mr. Winter felt that the gangster should take off his hat. He asked the first cameraman how he could give a note to Mr. Scorsese, and the first cameraman said, "I don't know. No one's ever given him a note before."[89]

• Film director Terry Gilliam has had hits with *The Fisher King* and *Twelve Monkeys*, but he also has had misses with movies such as the 2006 fantasy *Tideland*, which made only $66,453, perhaps because it starred the excellent actor Jeff Bridges as a decomposing corpse.

Following the financial disaster of that movie, movie studios wanted nothing to do with Mr. Gilliam, and so he walked the street of New York City while holding this sign: "Studio-Less Film Maker. Family to Support. Will Direct For Food." By the way, Mr. Gilliam had a fantastic childhood growing up in Minnesota. He and his family lived in a house that his father, a carpenter, insulated. After the house acquired indoor plumbing, he and his father worked on the old outhouse, turning it into a three-story treehouse. During snowy winters, young Terry would often jump from the top story and try to grab onto telephone wires, but instead fall into ten feet of snow. He remembers that this experience was "fantastic!" He also built igloos—sometimes with unfortunate results. On one occasion, a neighbor's dog climbed on top of an igloo, urinated, and crashed through the roof on top of the people inside.[90]

• Quentin Tarantino is famous for his crime movies *Reservoir Dogs*, *Pulp Fiction*, and *Jackie Brown*. As the writer/director of these movies, he was able to draw to some extent on his personal history. (He once spent 10 days in jail because of the $7,000 he owed in unpaid parking tickets.) Many people wonder where Mr. Tarantino got the name for his hit movie, *Reservoir Dogs*. It comes from the days he spent as a video store clerk when people often asked for Louis Malle's *Au Revoir les Enfants*. Mr. Tarantino had difficulty pronouncing the name, so he ended up calling it *Reservoir Dogs*. In an attempt to break into Hollywood, Mr. Tarantino falsified his resume, claiming that he had acted in Jean-Luc Godard's *King Lear*. Why that particular film? He guessed that the Hollywood figures in charge of hiring would not be familiar with it.[91]

• Supposedly, movie director Alfred Hitchcock once said that actors are cattle. Hearing that, Carole Lombard brought three cows to the set of *Mr. and Mrs. Smith* and hung name tags around their necks. The name tags said, "Carole Lombard," "Robert Montgomery," and "Gene Raymond." However, Mr. Hitchcock denied that he had ever said that actors were cattle, explaining, "I would never be capable of such a thoughtless, rude, and unfeeling remark ... what I probably said was that actors should be treated like cattle."[92]

• In Alfred Hitchcock's *Notorious* is a sequence in which characters played by Cary Grant and Ingrid Bergman hug and kiss in an uninterrupted shot that shows them going from a balcony to inside an apartment to answer a telephone. The sequence was based on real life. Mr. Hitchcock had once witnessed a young couple who walked across a field, holding on to each other even when the young man paused to urinate by a barn. Mr. Hitchcock says, "Love must not be interrupted—even for urination!"[93]

• Many people feel strongly about movies. When Western film maker John Ford died, some film scholars, including Jim Agnew and Alex Ameripoor, drove to Los Angeles to visit his grave, where they stood and sang, "Shall We Gather at the River," a song which is often sung in funerals in Western movies.[94]

• Comedian Charlie Chaplain directed many of his own movies. Once, he was told that his placement of the movie camera resulted in shots that were not interesting. He replied, "They don't have to be—*I* am interesting."[95]

Education

• In the 2009-2010 academic year, actor Tony Danza, who has a college degree in education, but not a teaching license, began teaching a sophomore English course at Northeast High School in Philadelphia, PA, as part of an A&E reality series called *Teach*. Because he did not have a teaching certificate, another teacher was always present in the one course that Mr. Danza taught, but fortunately the other teacher mostly observed and seldom needed to take over for Mr. Danza. As you may expect, Mr. Danza occasionally made mistakes. He said that he cried three times his first week of teaching. He once made a mistake when he tried to explain the role of the omniscient narrator, and one of his students corrected him. After that, he said that he was tempted to telephone every teacher that he had ever had and tell them that he had not realized how difficult teaching is. Mr. Danza also ran into non-teaching problems. Once he got down on his hands and knees and washed the floor of his classroom because it was not clean enough for him. Mr. Danza really did teach, guiding his students through such works of literature as *Romeo and Juliet*, *To Kill a Mockingbird*, and *Of Mice and Men*. The school district had to decide whether to renew Mr. Danza's contract partway through the school year. Because his students had made good academic progress, the district did renew his contract. Mr. Danza and the production company benefited the high school and the school district financially, paying it $3,500 for each episode (13 episodes in all) and paying for some expenses, as well as air-conditioning the library and donating money to the school uniform fund and the band and the choir. In addition, it put on "ExtravaDanza," a song-and-dance benefit that raised $12,000 for the school district.[96]

• In the 1960s, David Zucker attended school in Milwaukee. Occasionally, he was a class clown, and a teacher once told him, "I know one day I'll be paying good money to see you make me laugh, but right now, get your *ss back in that chair and crack that book!" Later, Mr. Zucker co-directed and co-wrote *Airplane!*[97]

• Maria Elena Salinas is a TV news anchor and a columnist. Her father is an intellectual who has influenced her. He knows six languages and has a doctorate degree in philosophy; in addition, he always carries a book with him. She once asked him what he was doing, and he replied, "Studying." She asked, "Studying at your age?" He replied, "Of course. You never stop learning.[98]

• Comedian and TV game-show host Jan Murray always regretted not graduating from high school; therefore, when he was in his 40s, he finally earned his high-school diploma. Afterwards, he joked, "How old can I be? I just graduated from high school!"[99]

Emmys

• In 1986, Marlo Thomas was nominated for an Emmy for Best Dramatic Actress for her performance in the TV movie *Nobody's Child*.

In the same year, *The Golden Girls*, a TV series produced by Tony Thomas, her brother, was nominated for Best Comedy Series. Their parents, comedian Danny Thomas and Rose Marie Thomas, decided not to attend the Emmy Awards that year because they knew that they would be devastated if one of their children won an Emmy and the other lost, so they watched the awards program on TV. A neighbor, Ted Mann, had a satellite dish with a feed from the East Coast, so when he was watching the middle of the Emmy Awards show other people on the West Coast, such as the Thomases, were watching the beginning. Mr. Mann called the Thomases with good news: "Tony just won the Emmy!" This was good news, and the Thomases threw coats over their pajamas and went to Mr. Mann's house to watch the rest of the Emmy Awards show. More good news: Marlo won the Emmy. The Thomases then got dressed up so they could celebrate that night with Tony and Marlo.[100]

• Tim Conway's speeches after winning an Emmy are great because he never talks about the Emmy Awards. Once, he thanked all the Tarzana Pitch 'n' Putt employees and recommended that everyone in the audience play golf there for an evening of relaxation.[101]

Chapter 3: From Fame to Hot Weather

Fame

• Christopher McDonald played Thelma's husband—make that repulsive husband—in *Thelma and Louise*. When the movie first appeared in theaters, he was recognized as he was driving down the street. A woman in the car next to him saw him and said, "Omigod, it's that guy from *Thelma and Louise*! Omigod!" The other woman in the car looked over and said, "Shoot him!"[102]

Fans

• African-American actress Nichelle Nichols is most famous for playing communications officer Uhura on the TV series *Star Trek* and in many movies, but she wanted to leave the series after only one season because she was most interested in performing musical theater. After getting some offers to perform in musical theater, she met with series creator Gene Roddenberry to tell him that she was considering leaving *Star Trek*, and he told her, "You can't do this. Don't you realize what I'm trying to get done here?" He then added, "OK, take the weekend and think about it and if you still feel that way Monday morning you'll go with my blessings." The following day she went to an NAACP fundraiser, where she met a special *Star Trek* fan: Dr. Martin Luther King, Jr., who told her, "I am the biggest Trekkie on the planet." After she told him that she was thinking of leaving the series, he urged her to stay, saying, "You cannot leave. [...] It's part of history now. This man has made this show that projects 300 years from now. This is who we are and we are beginning here, and you're representing us. You cannot leave because nobody can replace you. Only you." Ms. Nichols said, "I changed my mind right there because I was ordered. That was my leader. He said lots more. *Star Trek* was the only series that he and his wife, Coretta, would allow the children to stay up to see. And I was their hero. I could do nothing but Monday morning go in and tell Gene

Roddenberry what Dr. King had said, and if he still wanted me, I would stay. And I stayed and never looked back."[103]

• Comic actress Carol Burnett once attended a party, and she was surprised when Cary Grant, the Brad Pitt/ Hugh Grant of his day, showed up. Carol was such a big fan that she knew that if she actually met Mr. Grant, she would say something embarrassing, so she decided that she and her husband, Joe, should leave the party immediately, even though she knew that Mr. Grant was a fan of her variety show. Her husband protested, but she explained, "Poor Joe, you just don't get it. Look, he *likes* me! He makes it a point to watch our show every single week! You think I want to spoil that?" Unfortunately, Carol and her husband did not leave the party fast enough. Carol was introduced to Mr. Grant, who was—as always—charming—and she said the only thing she could think of to say to him: "You're a credit to your profession." Carol asks now, "Why didn't the floor open up?" While they were going back home, Joe thought about how Carol had been afraid that if she met Mr. Grant, she would say something embarrassing, and he told her, "You were right."[104]

• Jamie Farr, who played Klinger on *M*A*S*H*, gets many requests for autographs, sometimes when such requests ought not to be made—while eating in a restaurant with his wife, for example. Once, in Edmonton, Canada, a woman came up to while he was eating in a restaurant with his wife and asked him to sign her bra. Mr. Farr winked at his well-endowed wife and then looked back at the woman and said, "Sorry, I write bigger than that." Chestfallen—er, crestfallen—the woman left. By the way, at a charity function, the Farrs met Secretary of State Henry Kissinger. Mrs. Farr—Joy—was wearing an elegant black dress with a plunging neckline, and Mr. Kissinger stared at her cleavage. He said, "Hello, Mrs. Farr. So nice to meet you." She replied, "Nice meeting you, Henry." Later, Jamie said to Joy, "I call him Mr. Kissinger, or Mr. Secretary. How in the world can you call him Henry?" Joy replied, "Jamie, if he can look at my tits, I can call him Henry."[105]

• Rita Moreno's daughter loved *Sesame Street*, and when Ms. Moreno was offered a job as a cast member on the TV children's program *The Electric Company*, she took it. Today, many people remember her opening yell on the show: "Hey, you guys!" In 2008, she walked into a restaurant, and she heard a balding man with a fat stomach who had apparently grown up watching the show say, "Hey, you guys!" She immediately thought, "I can't be that old!" Ms. Moreno loved the Muppets on *Sesame Street*, and seeing Muppets creator Jim Henson in a restaurant one day, she got down on her knees before him, kissed his hand, and said, "Anything you want me to do on your show, I will do it. I can do all these little girl voices." He was embarrassed by the kiss, but excited by her offer to do voices for the Muppets. Ms. Moreno says, "And so I wound up doing the voice for several of the puppets, working with Frank Oz. It was so marvelous."[106]

• Celebrities frequently are fans of other celebrities. When Jennifer Love Hewitt was a teenager starring in the TV series *Party of Five*, she had a crush on fellow actor Johnny Depp, who stopped by the set one day when Love (as she is called) was not wearing makeup. Feeling the opposite of beautiful, Love screamed, ran away, and locked herself in a trailer until Mr. Depp had left. (Mr. Depp, a considerate man, later sent her flowers when she graduated from high school.) When Love used some of her earnings from *Party of Five* to buy a house, a young girl on a bicycle saw her moving in. Recognizing her, the excited young girl said, "Oh, my God! A celebrity is moving into my neighborhood!" Also excited, Love looked up the street and said, "Oh, my God! Where?" [107]

• Walt Disney was called Walt by pretty much everybody. At a restaurant in Disneyland, a waitress said to him, "Can I help you, Mr. Disney?" Walt replied, "Yes, but remember—I'm Walt. There's only one Mister at Disneyland, and that's *Mr.* Toad." Of course, he was famous, as was his friend Art Linkletter. Once, he and Art walked around Disneyland while wearing beards to disguise themselves. Art remembers, "The funny thing was, we were walking along and people were still coming us to us and asking for our autographs, and not one of them even asked, "Why are you wearing a beard?"[108]

• Many people love celebrities—and celebrity souvenirs. Barbra Streisand wore some earrings in *Funny Girl* but somehow they turned up missing. Over thirty years later, she rented a boat in Mexico, and she discovered that the boat owner's mother had the earrings, which were fake. Barbra had needed a fur coat cleaned, the earrings were in a pocket, and the boat owner's mother had kept them. Barbra asked, "Can you give them back? It's more than thirty years later, and you know, *they're mine.*" She never did get them back.[109]

• People sometimes act strangely around celebrities. Robert Mitchum once got on an elevator on which was a woman who recognized him, but found that she was unable to look him in the face. Instead, she stared at his tie. When Mr. Mitchum got off the elevator, he asked her, "Thunderstruck? Or just like the tie?"[110]

• After Sarah Michelle Gellar became famous as Buffy in TV's *Buffy the Vampire Slayer*, she had to change her life. For example, she put a fake name on her luggage so that overly obsessive fans would not steal it. And after being recognized in a restaurant, she once had to escape fans by fleeing by way of a loading dock.[111]

• In the comments section for a video clip from the Disney animated feature film *Beauty and the Beast* in which Angela Lansbury sings the theme song, someone who uses the moniker "MrSinister1979" wrote, "I watched this with my girlfriend last night. Kinda embarrassing, though, since I cried and she didn't."[112]

• Comedian Jay Leno once appeared on *Oprah Winfrey*, and afterward, he met a lot of enthusiastic male fans who escorted him to his car. Later, he discovered that the enthusiastic fans were also going on *Oprah Winfrey*—each of them had murdered his wife.[113]

• Her fans never felt that comedian Carol Burnett put on airs. Instead, she was like the fans themselves. One woman even told her, "I just love you. You're so common." According to Ms. Burnett, "I'm like your mother, your sister."[114]

• During the 1950s, comedian Sid Caesar, star of *Your Show of Shows*, was so famous that when he ate fast food people would steal French fries from his plate to take home as souvenirs.[115]

Fathers

• When actor/producer Ashton Kutcher was a teenager growing up in small-town Iowa, he was annoyed because it seemed to him that everyone's entertainment consisted of listening to police scanners. He says, "My parents knew if I'd been caught speeding before I even walked in the door." Of course, Ashton grew up and became a father himself. When he married actress Demi Moore, he became the father—along with their biological father Bruce Willis—of her three daughters. The three girls call Ashton "MOD," which is short for "My Other Dad." [116]

• Bill Cosby created the character of Fat Albert, and when *Fat Albert and the Cosby Kids* became an animated TV series, Mr. Cosby did the voice of Fat Albert. One day, he took his young son, Ennis, to the TV studio, where Ennis was shocked to discover that his father did the voice of Fat Albert. He said, "Dad, you mean *you're* Fat Albert?" [117]

• A man who had fathered 16 children once appeared on *You Bet Your Life*. Groucho Marx asked, "Why do you have so many children?" The man answered, "Because I like my wife." Groucho took a drag on his cigar, and then said, "I like my cigar, too, but I take it out sometime." [118]

Food

• In season seven of its nine seasons, Roseanne Barr's hit TV series *Roseanne* dropped out of the top 10, and suddenly she could no longer get reservations at fancy restaurants. She had her assistant call the Palm restaurant for a reservation that night, but she was told that they were full. Roseanne then had her assistant disguise her voice and call back to ask for a reservation that night for Tom Cruise and his then-wife Nicole Kidman, and—no surprise—the Palm was not full. The assistant made the reservation for 8 p.m., but as ordered by Roseanne she called back at 7:55 p.m. to say that Tom and Nicole would not be dining at the Palm because they had accepted an invitation from Roseanne to dine at a Denny's.[119]

• Andrew Zimmern hosts a TV show called *Bizarre Foods* on the Travel Channel. As you would expect, he eats a lot of bizarre foods—foods more bizarre than chocolate-covered crickets—on the show. The show is entertaining and family friendly, and one of its byproducts is that it teaches kids to be more open-minded about food. Each week, Mr. Zimmern says that he gets a few letters that basically say this: "My kids ate chicken nuggets and PB&J, and then we started watching your show, and we said to him over one dinner, 'Well, Mr. Zimmern would eat it.' And that just started him off. He started shoving everything he could into his mouth." Mr. Zimmern says, "I just think that's fantastic."[120]

• Dane Boedigheimer created *The Annoying Orange*, a very popular series of YouTube videos in which an orange insults its guests on a talk show. The videos end with a knife slicing the guest in two. He also created a parody of the horror film *The Ring*—Mr. Boedigheimer's version is titled *The Onion Ring*. He sent the video out in a mass email and told the recipients to send the video to five of their friends, threatening that if they did not, he would turn the recipients into onion rings. Unfortunately, an 11-year-old girl got the email and was terrified by it. Her mother emailed Mr. Boedigheimer, and he then emailed the 11-year-girl and assured her that he had no intention of turning her into food.[121]

• French New Wave film director Claude Chabrol, auteur of *Le Beau Serge* (1957) and *Les Biches* (1968), was an expert in fine food and fine wine. In fact, he sometimes chose the locations of his films partly on the basis of which restaurants were nearby. He once said, "If you have two possibilities, it would be cretinous not to choose the one where you eat best." When Mr. Chabrol died, Socialist party leader Martine Aubry said, "Chabrol was part of my daily life. Like many French people, I waited eagerly for the annual 'Chabrol.'"[122]

• After her parents divorced, Sarah Michelle Gellar of *Buffy the Vampire Slayer* fame was raised by her mother. She and her mother—a kindergarten teacher—struggled financially for a while. They used to joke that they ate pasta six days a week—then splurged on Friday night when they ate macaroni and cheese. Now, of course, they eat much better.[123]

• *The Garry Moore Show*, which was popular in the 1950s, used to occasionally feature exotic foods, which Mr. Moore and his guests would sample. On one show, Mr. Moore told guest Wally Cox, who was somewhat hesitant to sample the delicacies, "Wally, if you don't eat your French-fried grasshoppers, you won't get any chocolate-covered ants."[124]

Friends

• Mel Blanc, the voice of such cartoon characters as Bugs Bunny, Elmer Fudd, and Daffy Duck, once was caught speeding. He was not speeding on purpose. He liked good cars, and he explains, "The car, a brand-new Rolls Royce, handled so smoothly I hadn't even realized I was speeding." Of course, the police officer asked for his driver license, and recognizing the name, asked, "Are you *the* Mel Blanc?" Mr. Blanc replied—using Bugs Bunny's voice—that yes, he was. The police officer grinned and said, "Well, I guess I'm going to have to let you off with a warning. My kids would never forgive me if I gave a ticket to Bugs Bunny." Bugs also saved Mr. Blanc in a much more serious situation. On 24 January 1961 he was involved in a very bad two-car accident—the fault of the other driver—and was in a coma for three weeks. People kept saying his name to him, but he never responded. On Valentine's Day, a cartoon starring Bugs Bunny was playing on the TV, and his doctor, Louis Conway, said to him, "How are you feeling today, Bugs?" Mr. Blanc has no memory of this, but witnesses say that he came out of the coma and replied in Bugs' voice, very weakly, "Eh, just fine, Doc. How're you?" One of the people who kept Mr. Blanc laughing during the months of recovery was one of his employers, Jack Benny, a comedian who got laughs by pretending to be a cheapskate. In the hospital Mr. Benny once gave Mr. Blanc one-half of a candy bar, saying, "I didn't think you were in shape to eat the whole thing, so why waste it?" (By the way, Mel's son, Noel, got his name in honor of his grandfather, Grandpa Nachum, who had been renamed Nolan when he came to the United States. Because someone else had recently been named Nolan in the grandfather's honor, the Blancs searched for a name variant they liked, deciding on Noel in part because of Noel Coward. Afterward, they realized that Noel Blanc means "White Christmas" in French, which is a strange name for a Jewish kid.) Mr. Blanc also received another gift, this one from Warner's: a 3-foot-high card depicting 14 of the cartoon characters he voiced. Their doctor was saying to a nurse, "It's a baffling case, nurse. They all seem to have temporarily lost their voices." Mr. Blanc recovered from the accident and gave voice to cartoon characters until the year 1989, when he died at age 81.[125]

• So what are the lives of the rich and famous really like? One day, world-famous movie star Gwyneth Paltrow was driving in a car with her friend the world-famous make-up artist Kevyn Aucoin. Unfortunately, Gwyneth's butt fell asleep, so she told her friend, "Kevyn, you have to punch me in the ass because I can't sit here anymore. I can't feel my ass." She pulled herself up on the steering wheel, and Kevyn obligingly punched her butt a few times. They then noticed a van filled with guys in the next lane looking at them and wondering what was going on. Both Gwyneth and Kevyn started laughing so hard that, Gwyneth says, "We were, like, 'Oh, my God, we're going to pee in the car.'" Another time, Kevyn got trapped in an elevator and could not get out for almost an hour. He hated it, but fortunately the world-famous movie star Sharon Stone, one of his friends, learned of his plight and lay on the floor outside the elevator so she could talk to him through a crack and keep him from having a nervous breakdown. Sharon says, "You know, he always tried to cram too much into each day, so he always had millions of excuses for why he was late. But this excuse was for real!"[126]

Gays and Lesbians

• Celebrity publicist Howard Bragman has helped a number of actors and athletes come out of the closet. One of the actors was Dick Sargent, who played the second Darren on the TV sitcom *Bewitched*. After Mr. Sargent made his decision to come out, Mr. Bragman arranged for *Entertainment Tonight* to interview him. This made Mr. Sargent laugh because he figured that *Entertainment Tonight* would not be interested; after all, it had been years since he had been on TV. However, *Entertainment Tonight* was interested, and after the interview appeared, Mr. Sargent received many, many letters thanking him for coming out of the closet and living his life honestly. In addition, he started getting a lot more acting jobs. Mr. Bragman says, "Typically, when actors come out, good things happen. In fact, every person I worked with who came out ended up happier in their new life."[127]

• Scott Evans played a gay character in the soap opera *One Life to Live*; he is gay in real life. On the soap opera, his character's coming out led to a lot of anguish; in real life, his coming out did not. When he told his mother, Lisa, that he was gay, she replied, "Cool. What do you want for dinner?" Actually, according to Lisa, she always knew that her son was gay. A family story is that when Scott was born, Lisa looked at him and said, "Oh, yay. I got a gay one." Scott also came out to Chris, his brother. Chris told him, "I am a little p*ssed." Scott asked, "Why?" Chris said, "You told everyone else six months ago. Why did it take you so long?" Now Scott remembers, "I was terrified to tell him. I look back on it now kind of laughing hysterically, thinking that I thought I couldn't."[128]

• Gay visibility is important in combating homophobia. Quite simply, when straight people meet and know gay people, they realize that gay people are much like other people and should not be loathed or feared. Neil Patrick Harris and George Takei are two out actors who have appeared on radio's *The Howard Stern Show*, which from 2001 to 2009 had Artie Lange as a cast member. Mr. Lange has sometimes described himself as a homophobe (at least in his act), but he has learned a lot about gay people from meeting and talking with Mr. Harris and Mr. Takei. Mr. Lange says, "I joke around about this stuff a lot and talk about it in my act, but I'm being dead honest right now. If my son ever [told me he was gay], the first thing I would do would be to give him a hug and tell him there was no way I have a problem with this and I love you."[129]

• In 2008, George Takei (the actor who played Sulu on the original TV series of *Star Trek*) and Brad Altman got engaged to be married. Both of them were eagerly awaiting a ruling on same-sex marriage from the California Supreme Court and both of them were expecting the ruling to be favorable, so they kept their TV constantly tuned to CNN. When the ruling legalizing same-sex marriage was announced, Mr. Takai was eating a sandwich. Mr. Altman dropped on his knees in front of his long-time (more than 21 years!) partner and asked, "George, will you marry me?" Mr. Takei, who would have been on his knees first if not hampered by the sandwich, replied, "Darn it! You beat me to it. I was going to ask you."[130]

• Max Mutchnick, gay co-creator of the TV series *Will & Grace*, featuring gay characters Will Truman and Jack McFarland, has a voice that leads to interesting conversations with telephone operators. For example, he will make a call to information and hear, "Hello. This is information. How can I help you?" He replies, "I'd like the Paramount Theater on Main Street." The telephone operator then says, "There is no Paramount Theater [on Main Street], Ma'am." He then says, "I'm not a ma'am." And the telephone operator says, "I didn't call you a man, Miss." This frequently happens to Mr. Mutchnick, who says, "I keep having this exchange over and over again."[131]

• In Great Britain, a radio show titled *Writing the Century* is based on the diaries and letters of real people from the fairly recent past. One episode focused on Steven, who in the late 1970s was an 18-year-old gay man whose best friends dressed like girls and used the names Chrissy and Gloria. One day, Chrissy and Gloria visited a jobs centre, and the interviewer asked whether they really thought that they would get jobs dressed "like that." Chrissy and Gloria asked, "Like what?" The interviewer replied, "High heels and red plastic trousers."[132]

• David Moretti, an actor in the TV series *The Lair*, was very worried about coming out to his father. But he told him, and he waited for his reaction. All his father said was this: "Wow—hey, can I still get grandkids?" This was a relief to David, who says, "All I could do was laugh. He was a progressive liberal alpha Italian—who knew! He completely deflated the 'situation' with one sentence. I told him that kids were definitely a possibility, just not sure how soon. We later had lunch, and that was that. I was a very fortunate kid."[133]

• Gay British television celebrity Dale Winton once walked past a pub only to hear a hooligan in a pack of hooligans yell at him, "Poof! F**king queer!" He thought about walking away, but instead he turned, went up to the hooligans, smiled, and asked, "Who said it? Who said that? Who called me a f**king poof? I want to know." Finally, one of the hooligans admitted calling him that. Mr. Winton then said, "You're absolutely right, you win a tenner. Have a drink."[134]

• Gays Stan Zimmerman and Jim Berg have written for *The Golden Girls* and *Roseanne*, as well as for their own Lifetime sitcom, *Rita Rocks*. While working on a script for *Rita Rocks*, they discovered that all the straight men on their staff had held a discussion about who they would sleep with if they were gay: Stan or Jim? Jim says, "He got the executive producer, but I got the hotter writers—so it all worked out."[135]

Gifts

• Ed McMahon hosted *Star Search* for a long time. Occasionally, the contestants were children, and he worried about disappointing them. Once, the two finalists were 12-year-old Mary Johnson and five-year-old Allison Porter. Mr. McMahon did not know who the judges would pick to win, but he worried that young Allison might lose. He said to the show's producers, "This is just awful. You've got to give me something to give to the five-year-old if she doesn't win. Get me a big stuffed animal or something. The 12-year-old won, and Mr. McMahon said, "Mary gets the one hundred thousand dollars!" Then he said to Allison, "Look what we have for you!" Allison got a big stuffed panda that was almost as big as she was—she was thrilled and Ed was relieved.[136]

• Mary Richards, the character Mary Tyler Moore played on *The Mary Tyler Moore Show*, had a big M hanging on a wall of her apartment. After the TV series ended, Ms. Moore kept the M. Eventually, she gave it away to be sold at a charity fundraiser. Her husband, cardiologist S. Robert Levine, bought it and gave it back to her. By the way, Mary Tyler Moore started using her middle name professionally when she registered with the Actors Equity Association. This union already had five Mary Moores as members.[137]

• Gossip columnist Hedda Hopper was widely despised. For her birthday one year, actress Joan Bennett sent her a very special gift: a skunk that had been dead for a week. Enclosed with the gift was this note: "Happy birthday, dear. [Signed] Joan."[138]

Girlfriends

• When Ashton Kutcher, one of the stars of *That 70s Show*, was growing up, his older sister, Tausha, played practical jokes on him. For example, she would put make-up on him as he slept. Ashton says, "Can you imagine how scary that was for a little kid, to wake up with lipstick, eye shadow and mascara?" Of course, he grew up and had girlfriends, both for real and on the movie screen. For example, Piper Perabo played his girlfriend in the movie *Cheaper By the Dozen*. When she met Ashton's real-life girlfriend, Demi Moore, on the set, she said, "Hi, you're gorgeous! I'll be kissing your boyfriend in about 10 minutes." Ms. Moore, who has kissed several actors in her own movies, was amused.[139]

Golf

• Actor Jim Backus, co-star of the TV sitcom *I Married Joan*, was friends with women's champion golfer Babe Zaharias. He also knew Katherine Hepburn. One day they were all on the golf course, and Humphrey Bogart, with whom Ms. Hepburn had just finished acting in *The African Queen*, came riding up to them in a limo. (Yes, the limo was on the fairways.) Ms. Hepburn said, "Look, there's Bogie!" Babe spun around and told her, "Lady, never say that word on a golf course." (A bogie is one over par.) After Babe died of cancer, Mr. Backus played golf with her husband, who presented him with a golf club that Babe had used and that Babe wanted Mr. Backus to have. Mr. Backus prized that club. It still had little tufts of drying grass on it, along with a little sod and a white mark where she had last hit the ball. Mr. Backus carried it home and made mental preparations to have the club encased in glass the next day to preserve the tufts of drying grass, the little bit of sod, and the white mark. He got up the next morning and checked on the golf club. It was different. His maid walked into the room and said, "Isn't it beautiful, Mr. Backus! I cleaned and polished it real good!" Mr. Backus almost cried.[140]

Good Deeds

• For a while, Michael Moore, who now directs documentaries, published an investigative newspaper in Flint, Michigan: the *Flint Voice*. Some of the investigative stories, such as exposing racism in businesses, resulted in a major lack of advertising revenue, and so getting enough money for the newspaper was difficult. One person who helped start the newspaper and supported it until his death was folksinger Harry Chapin. After a Harry Chapin concert, Mr. Moore went backstage to see him. A security guard asked him what was doing, and Mr. Moore replied, "I'm just stopping by to see Harry." The security guard replied, "The hell you are!" But Mr. Chapin appeared at his dressing room and decided to see Mr. Moore, who told him that he and some friends wanted to start an alternative newspaper and asked him to please do a benefit concert for them. Mr. Chapin listened to Mr. Moore's plans for the newspaper and said, "Sounds like a worthy effort. Here's my manager's number. Give him a call and I'll see what I can do." A few months later, he did a sold-out benefit concert, and Mr. Moore and his friends started the newspaper. Mr. Chapin then did annual benefit concerts for the next five years until his death in an accident on the Long Island Expressway in July 1981. Mr. Moore kept the newspaper going until 1985, when he shut it down to become editor of *Mother Jones*, which turned out to be a bad idea. He has never forgotten Mr. Chapin's generosity.[141]

• Despite good intentions, not all would-be good deeds work out. In 2009, actress Anne Hathaway saw a shabbily dressed woman sitting on a bench at a bus stop. Thinking that the woman was homeless, she offered her a doggy bag of leftovers—gourmet leftovers. Rather than being pleased, the woman was outraged: "What do you think I am—HOMELESS? ... I'm just waiting for the bus! ... Just because I'm not all dressed up, you think I'm a homeless woman?" Ms. Hathaway apologized and left. (She does get credit for her attempt at a good deed.) Other good deeds do work out, but they are not rewarded. In 2010, Keifer Sutherland, who served 30 days in jail in 2008 for DUI and gained several IQ points as a result (he now has a chauffeur when he drinks), left Hollywood's Piano Bar and saw an attendant urging an insistent drunken man not to drive. Mr. Sutherland walked over to the drunken man and spent 15 minutes talking to him before convincing him to accept a ride home in his limo. He then gave the man a ride home, going approximately 45 minutes out of his way to do so. Unfortunately, when he and his driver delivered the drunken man home, the drunken man's wife thought that they were her husband's drinking buddies and strongly criticized them for being a bad influence on her husband. Here's a third deed by a movie star: in 2005 Jessica Alba boarded a plane whose take-off was delayed because a plus-size passenger could not fit his butt into his seat in coach. Ms. Alba paid the money for the man's ticket to be upgraded to first-class, so that he would have a wider seat. (She did not want him to be told about her good deed.)[142]

• Johnny Carson respected stand-up comedians, and when he felt that they were ready to get the very important exposure that *The Tonight Show* could provide, he tried to make their very first appearance a success. When a new comedian would appear on *The Tonight Show*, he or she would come on after a commercial break, and Johnny would always say, "We're back now, and I'm glad you're in such a good mood tonight because my next guest is making his first appearance on *The Tonight Show*." This was a subtle way of helping the comedian. After all, if the comedian thinks that the audience is in a good mood, the comedian is much more likely to be a success. In addition, by letting the audience know that this is the comedian's first appearance, Johnny helps the audience to be on the side of the comedian—I think that most audience members would want a first-timer to succeed. Tom Dreeson remembers what Johnny would say for Tom's (and other comedians') first appearance on *The Tonight Show*: "You'd hear that for every comedian the first time. And he only did it the first time."[143]

• Latino comedian George Lopez was greatly influenced and inspired by Freddie Prinze, Sr., a Latino comedian who starred in the TV series *Chico and the Man*. After Mr. Lopez moved into a house near Mr. Prinze's widow, Kathy, she gave him a keychain that her late husband had owned. This keyring became a good-luck charm that Mr.

Lopez put into his pants pocket each time he began to film an episode of his sitcom, *The George Lopez Show*. Mr. Lopez worked hard to get Mr. Prinze, who died at age 22 after shooting himself, the recognition he deserved, including a star on the Hollywood Walk of Fame. He also helped Mr. Prinze's son, Freddy Prinze, Jr., in his acting career, including getting a sitcom on ABC. Mr. Prinze, Jr., who when he was young had heard people say bad things about his father, said, "George Lopez says without Freddie Prinze [Sr.] there's no George Lopez. ... But without George Lopez, nobody says good stuff about my father. And the fact that he goes above and beyond to help me, after he's succeeded, that's a big deal to me."[144]

• Soupy Sales was on an airplane eating steak when he noticed another guy eating steak with steak sauce, so he asked the stewardess for steak sauce. Unfortunately, the guy had brought his own steak sauce in a little packet, and the airline did not serve steak sauce. Soupy wrote a letter to the airline suggesting that they serve steak sauce with their steak, and the airline was nice enough to send him a bunch of packets of steak sauce. The next time Soupy boarded a plane and ate steak, he was prepared. He put steak sauce on his steak, and he heard a fellow ask a stewardess for steak sauce. He also heard the stewardess explain that the airline didn't have steak sauce. No problem. Soupy had a bunch of steak-sauce packets in his pocket, and he shared them with other steak-eating passengers.[145]

• *The Big Bang Theory* is a popular television show in the United States, and audiences in Belarus started viewing their own knock-off version of the show in 2010. Unfortunately, the knock-off version was unlicensed. Also unfortunately, the TV production company of the unlicensed knockoff was owned by Belarus, and therefore *Big Bang Theory* co-creator Chuck Lorre could not sue the production company. He did put a title card in the show; the card stated that he hoped that Belarus would "send us some felt hats" as payment for stealing the program. Actually, the actors of the knock-off had believed that they were participating in a legal, licensed television show. When they found out that the show was unlicensed, they quit and the production company was forced to suspend the illegal program.[146]

• In 2001, in Toronto, Renee Zellweger saw a homeless man lying on a sidewalk on a cold winter day. She pulled her SUV over, walked over to the homeless man, and gave him her gloves. After chatting with him briefly, she went to a restaurant and ordered a hot take-out meal. The homeless man told his friends that a famous actress had given him the warm gloves, and an eyewitness related, "Renee walked right up to the homeless man and handed him the food she bought for him at the restaurant, and once again his face lit up with joy. The stranger's friends were so impressed by Renee's kindness they gave her a flower to take with her. Then they waved goodbye to Renee as she drove away, and huddled together to feast on the hot meal."[147]

• Before becoming a comedian, Jay Leno worked prepping fancy foreign cars in Boston. He often had to go to Rolls Royce headquarters in New York, and he would stop by the Improv in an attempt to get on stage and try to make people laugh. One day, he said to Improv owner Bud Friedman, "Mr. Friedman, my name is Jay Leno. This is the third night in a row I've driven down from Boston. I don't get on. When can I get on?" Mr. Friedman asked, "You drive down from Boston and back in one night?" Jay replied, "Yeah," and Mr. Friedman said, "You're on next."[148]

• When Mister Rogers was a small child, he sometimes used to watch the news on TV and see frightening things. Whenever this happened, his mother told him, "Look for the helpers. You will always find people who are helping."[149]

Hair

• Ed Sullivan, who was a columnist before becoming a TV personality, once wrote an item about comedian George Burns' use of a toupee. Mr. Burns was annoyed and told Mr. Sullivan off. Mr. Sullivan protested, "I didn't think you would mind." Mr. Burns replied, "If I didn't mind, why would I be wearing a toupee?"[150]

Halloween

• One Halloween, cartoon director Chuck Jones of Bugs Bunny fame ran out of treats—no candy, no apples, and no pennies. (This was a long time ago.) A little boy came up to his door and said, "Trick or treat." Since Chuck had no treats left, he told the boy, "Everything's gone—it'll have to be a trick." The little boy said, "All right," and he went out onto Chuck's lawn and stood on his head.[151]

Hot Weather

• George Tobias is famous for playing Abner, the husband of snoopy Mrs. Kravitz on TV's *Bewitched*. On Broadway, he played the part of the Russian dance teacher in the George S. Kaufman/Moss Hart hit *You Can't Take It With You*. All summer in sweltering New York City he grew a full beard for the role, only to be told later by Mr. Kaufman that all that was really needed was a goatee.[152]

Chapter 4: From Husbands and Wives to Practical Jokes

Husbands and Wives

• Filmmaker Alfred Hitchcock proposed to his future wife, Alma Reville, while she was seasick on a voyage. As Mr. Hitchcock told the story, he hoped that her resistance might be lowered by illness and thus she would be more inclined to say yes and marry him. Mr. Hitchcock said that when he asked her to marry him, "She groaned, nodded her head [yes], and burped. It was one of my greatest scenes — a little weak on dialogue, perhaps, but beautifully staged and not overplayed." They married in 1926, and Mr. Hitchcock said later, "She puts up with a lot from me. I dare say that any man who names his dog Phillip of Magnesia, as I did, is hard to live with." Mr. Hitchcock was noted for his many practical jokes. While filming *The 39 Steps*, a film that required the leading man and leading lady — Robert Donat and Madeleine Carroll — to be handcuffed, Mr. Hitchcock pretended that he could not find the key that would unlock the two. The handcuffs stayed on for another hour, but Mr. Donat and Ms. Carroll got along wonderfully. Some of the humor in Mr. Hitchcock's films comes from his cameos. In *Lifeboat*, most of the film takes place on a lifeboat at sea. Mr. Hitchcock appears in the Before and the After photos of a newspaper advertisement for Reduco, a weight-loss product. (Mr. Hitchcock had recently lost 100 pounds on a diet.) Mr. Hitchcock said, "I was literally submerged by letters from fat people who wanted to know where and how they could get Reduco." He once told some off-color jokes to some friends and then noticed that actress Grace Kelly was listening. He asked if she was shocked by the jokes, and she replied, "No. I went to a girls' convent school, Mr. Hitchcock; I heard all those things when I was 13." He was delighted by her answer.[153]

• Jeff Bridges does not consider himself good at romance. He does rub his wife's back, but he says that he knows that she deserves more than that. Still, he does carry a photograph that shows him talking to her for the first time ever. It happened in Montano, where Susan, who is now his wife, was a local girl. He saw her because she stood out; she was "gorgeous," he says, and she had a broken nose and two black eyes—the result of a car accident. Mr. Bridges says, "Somehow the bruises juxtaposed with that beauty were amazing. I couldn't take my eyes off her." He summoned his courage and asked her out, but she declined, and then she added, "It's a small town. Maybe I'll see you around." A couple of days later, they met again, and they ended up falling in love. Fifteen years later, Mr. Bridges opened up some mail from a make-up guy who had been working on that movie in Montana. The make-up guy had found and mailed to Mr. Bridges a photograph of him asking a pretty local girl on a date. Mr. Bridges says, "So I have a photo of the first words I ever said to my wife. It's unbelievable, and I always carry it around."[154]

• Latino comedian George Lopez and his manager, Ann Serrano, dated for a couple of years, and she was ready to get married. However, she realized that he was not going to propose to her, so she proposed to him—kind of. She said to him, "Guess who's getting married? ... Us." She gave him a memorable Valentine's Day present after they were married. When he was in high school, he had won a varsity letter in baseball, but he didn't have the money to get a jacket on which to sew the letter. Years later, she got him the jacket and had the letter sewed on. She gave it to him on the set of his sitcom, *The George Lopez Show*. Mr. Lopez remembers that he reacted in a memorable way: "Bawling my eyes out right there on Sound Stage 4, overwhelmed by an act so thoughtful and kind, symbolic of a healthy family relationship—wife, husband, and child—I'd never known except on TV."[155]

• Clark Gable was a ladies' man, but he wore dentures and they did not embarrass him. Hollywood scriptwriter Anita Loos remembers seeing Mr. Gable rinsing his dentures at an outdoor faucet. He looked at her, pointed to his caved-in mouth, and said, exaggerating a lisp, "Look! America's thweetheart!" One of Mr. Gable's wives was the comic actress Carole Lombard. Once, she was walking down the street and a man driving a truck offered her a lift. She accepted, and the man told her, "You remind me of Carole Lombard." Ms. Lombard pretended to be shocked and said, "If you compare me to that cheap floozy, I'll get right off your truck!" The man apologized to her.[156]

• Betty White, star of *The Mary Tyler Moore Show* and *Golden Girls*, was a career woman who took a long time to get married. At age 41, she finally said yes to the proposal of game-show host Allen Ludden, who for an entire year wore on a necklace around his neck the engagement ring he wanted to give her. They remained married until his death.[157]

Insults

• A burglar once broke into the home of cartoon director Chuck Jones of Bugs Bunny fame and stole some of his stuff, not including his drawings. Mr. Jones was a little insulted by this, but something even more insulting had happened to one of his painter friends: A burglar had broken into the painter's home, cut out the friend's paintings from their frames, and stolen the frames![158]

• Keith Olbermann of MSNBC *Countdown With Keith Olbermann* fame has a sharp mind, sharp wit, and sharp typing fingers. As you might expect, he gets a lot of hate e-mail, and on occasion he has responded—forcefully. To a hate e-mailer who wrote that his "hero" must be al-Qaida leader Abu Musab al-Zarqawi, Mr. Olbermann responded, "Hey, save the oxygen for somebody whose brain can use it. Kill yourself."[159]

Journalism

• National Public Radio commentator Daniel Schorr has had an extraordinarily long career, and he is still working hard in his 90s. Of course, in that time, he has experienced and been a part of much history, including being on President Richard M. Nixon's "enemies list." He says about his younger colleagues at NPR, "They frequently come to me and ask about Watergate. I've become 'Mr. History.'" Unfortunately, some of his younger colleagues have little sense of history. For example, Mr. Schorr tells a story about a person who said to him, "Daniel, I had a question. You covered the Spanish-American War and …"—of course, the Spanish-American War occurred in 1898, while Mr. Schorr was born in 1916. Mr. Schorr does, of course, use his knowledge of history in his work; he says that "one thing I consciously try to do in the commentaries is take today's development and stack it up against a history of what might have happened before."[160]

Language

• Comedy writer Treva Silverman got turned down for a job on Johnny Carson's show because, she was told, the men who worked there liked to curse and would not feel comfortable with a woman present. She did get a job on Carol Burnett's show *The Entertainers*, and at a meeting she remembered that she had been told that Johnny's male employees liked to curse, and so she cursed at the meeting — because she wanted Carol's male employees to feel comfortable. After a while, one of Carol's male employees said to her, "Treva, please don't curse. It makes me feel embarrassed." Treva says about Carol's male employees, "And really, everybody was very accepting and very nice."[161]

• In *The Exorcist*, 13-year-old Linda Blair played a character who uses horribly bad language referring to sexual acts. Many newspapers editorials were written against allowing a 13-year-old actress to use such language; however, Ms. Blair did not recite the lines. The really bad language was spoken by actress Mercedes McCambridge, whom Orson Welles had called "the world's greatest radio actress." She was also an excellent film actress, appearing in *Giant* and *Touch of Evil*.[162]

• My favorite sight gag on *The Bob Newhart Show* occurs when a black man with a huge dog walks out of Bob Hartley's office, then commands, "Sit, Whitey!" Dentist Jerry Robinson, a white man, immediately sits. The audience then learns that the black man had been talking to his dog, which was named "Whitey."[163]

• Kermit Schafer, collector of the funny misspeakings in broadcasting known as bloopers, once was in England, where BBC commentator Marion White told him that she had some "lovely boobs" to tell him about. That's when Mr. Schafer learned that in England bloopers are known as boobs.[164]

Letters

• Barbara Feldon, who played the role of Agent 99 on TV's *Get Smart*, is an original. She once had an oven that didn't work. Since she didn't cook anyway, she used the oven as a place to store her unanswered fan mail.[165]

Mishaps

• Frequently, the writers attended seminars for *The Andy Griffith Show*. Writers would toss out ideas for episodes, and at the end of the seminar executive producer Sheldon Leonard would assign story ideas to the writers. One such story idea became "The Pickle Story," in which Sheriff Andy Taylor and Deputy Sheriff Barney Fife substitute store-bought pickles for Aunt Bee's homemade "kerosene" pickles. At the story conference, writer Fred Fox desperately wanted to write "The Pickle Story," but because he stuttered, he remained silent, hoping his writing partner, Izzie Ellinson, would speak up. Unfortunately, when Mr. Leonard was allocating "The Pickle Story," Mr. Ellinson was busy looking over some notes, so the coveted story went to another writer. Mr. Fox stood up and shouted, "For G-g-g-god's sake, Izzie, you just b-b-b-blew 'The Pickle Story'!"[166]

• Jack Lemmon worked in the early days of live television, with its consequent mishaps. In one show, he and another actor were playing detectives, and the other actor was supposed to get shot, by not by Jack, who was supposed to shoot the bad guy. Unfortunately, Jack shot his blank gun right into his fellow detective's rear end. The "detective" shouted a string of profanity that ended up in ordinary USAmericans' living rooms. On another show, Jack was playing a surgeon. In one scene, he was supposed to ask for a hypodermic needle, but instead asked for a hypodeemic needle. This made the other actors laugh, including the actor who was supposed to be playing a heavily sedated patient.[167]

• As a young reporter, Connie Chung projected an image of self-confidence to other reporters, even at times when she ought not have. For example, in Russia a male reporter asked her how she was getting along with the Russian language. She replied that she was having no problems at all. He then asked her, "So what are you doing in the men's room?" In the United States, she once overslept and had to rush to a Senate judiciary hearing about Watergate. Because the elevator was broken, she was forced to run up several flights of stairs. After she arrived at her destination, a microphone was placed on her, but after running so much, all she could do was pant.[168]

• Actor Michael Landon seldom ate breakfast or lunch; instead, he would eat supper and often add a late-night snack. One night, at around 1 p.m. he made himself a plate of spaghetti and took it to his and his wife's bedroom, but discovered that he had forgotten the grated cheese. He put the plate of spaghetti, which was covered with tomato sauce, on the bed and left to get the grated cheese. His wife turned over in bed and woke up when her hand hit the plate of spaghetti. She turned on the light, looked at her hand, saw what she thought was blood, and started screaming. Michael ran to the bedroom and calmed her down.[169]

• When Piper Laurie was a young starlet, her studio sent her to many events. She says, "They were breaking me in, getting me used to people staring at me." One such event was a medical convention, where she was given a bag and told to help herself to the free goodies. She remembers, "They had all of these medical products. I walked around, and there was nothing that really appealed to me until I saw these little packages, which I thought maybe had bubble gum in them. So I just filled my bag with them. They were actually condoms. The publicity guy saw it with a mixture of hilarity and terror—he confiscated them." [170]

• Actor John Leguizamo grew up in Queens on Denman Street—by the elevated No. 7 train. This made watching mysteries on TV difficult. Mr. Leguizamo says, "As soon as they were about to reveal the killer, you'd hear, 'And the murderer is ...'"—and the train would go by and drown out the sound. He says, however, that he and his family grew skilled at reading lips.[171]

• In the late 1940s, Jimmy Crum frequently did "Man in the Street" interviews for a radio program sponsored by King's Shoe Store. During the interviews, Mr. Crum praised the shoe store. Unfortunately, during one interview, a woman listened to his praise, then snorted and said on the air, "I wouldn't go into that damn place if you paid me!"[172]

• A 1978 Benson & Hedges TV commercial was filmed in Death Valley, where the most recent rain had fallen in 1913. As soon as the production crew arrived to shoot the TV commercial, it rained nonstop for a week, costing a fortune as the crew sat around and waited for the rain to stop.[173]

• Joe E. Brown once guest hosted on a daytime talk show. He interviewed a woman with four children and said, "That's your entire family, I suppose." She replied, "Hell, no—there's a father, too."[174]

Money

• Jane Seymour is best known for starring in TV's *Dr. Quinn, Medicine Woman*, a series that fell to her by luck—bad luck. She was going through a divorce with a man who she says both cheated on her and messed up her finances in a major way. She points out, "I lost everything—I lost my homes, everything. So I totally understand people now who are losing their homes to the banks because I was THERE. It's devastating." In desperation, she called her agent and said, "I need to work yesterday." Her agent replied, "OK. That's interesting. Anything?" She confirmed, "Anything." A good agent, he started calling the television networks to let them know, "Jane will do anything but she's got to do it NOW." CBS replied, "We've got this movie called *Dr. Quinn, Medicine Woman*. We don't think it'll make it as a series, but in case it does, we need her to sign for five years. She has to start tomorrow morning at 5 a.m." She loved the script, the audience loved the movie, and she did 180 hours of the series, solving her financial crisis in a major way.[175]

• Early in his career, Bill Hanna of Hanna-Barbera cartoon fame, worked for Harman-Ising, which—of course—made cartoons. By his third year, he had some responsibility—he was the head of the inking and painting department—and he was making $37.50 per week. But then one of his bosses, Rudy Ising, hired his girlfriend to work for Mr. Hanna in a job with less responsibility—at $60 a week. Mr. Hanna got really angry, and he headed over to the Disney Studio to ask Walk Disney for a job. Mr. Disney listened to Mr. Hanna and said, "I'll tell you, Bill, we already have a girl in our inking and painting department who's doing a h*ll of a good job. I suggest that you go back and tell Rudy about your problem and I'll bet that you get your money." Mr. Hanna did go back, and he thinks that Mr. Disney telephoned Mr. Ising and talked to him because Mr. Ising immediately walked into his office and said, "Bill, you're going to get your raise. From now on, you'll be drawing sixty dollars a week."[176]

• Joseph Barbera's wife, Sheila, came up with the idea to have Fred and Wilma Flintstone of the cartoon *Flintstones* have a baby. Mr. Barbera liked the idea and attended two days of meetings in which it was decided that the Flintstones should have a baby boy. Shortly afterward, he received a call from Ed Justin, who handled Hanna-Barbera merchandising in New York. Mr. Justin said, "I hear the Flintstones are having a baby." Then he asked, "Boy or girl?" Hearing the answer, "It's a boy! Fred, Jr.—a chip off the old rock," Mr. Justin said, "That's too bad. I've got the Vice President of Ideal Toy here, and the only dolls they're doing are girls. We could have had a hell of a deal if it had been a girl." Mr. Barbera immediately said, "It's a girl. Her name is ... Pebbles. A pebble off the old rock." Mr. Barbera pointed out, "Some ideas develop after days of meetings. Others are born in the flash of a dollar sign set off by a single phone call."[177]

• Many people do ultra-cheap Web-based series of ultra-cheap entertainment. For example, Stacie Ponder, a freelance writer for <AfterEllen.com> (under the name Final Girl), created the horror series *Ghostella's Haunted Tomb* with a budget of, she estimates, 49 cents. So how do you make a Web-based series for 49 cents? Ms. Ponder says that it helps to have a roommate (Heidi Martinuzzi) who is willing to star in the series. In addition, many people are willing to create their own costumes and volunteer their time so they can appear in the series. And it helps to have a mother who is willing to contribute the 49 cents. Of course, 49 cents does not go very far, and Ms. Ponder found herself eating a lot of mustard sandwiches. Making the Web-based series is both fun and educational, and here are a few things that Ms. Ponder has learned: "People can be extremely cool and helpful if you just ask, "[…] a great recipe for homemade fake blood," and "All things considered, mustard sandwiches really aren't that bad."[178]

• During the writers' strike of 2007-2008, Tim Long, writer and executive producer on *The Simpsons*, became a USAmerican citizen. At the citizenship ceremony, he met and introduced himself to an older gentleman from Guatemala who asked him to explain why the writers were striking. Of course, Mr. Long did that, using such terms as "streaming rights" and "residuals" and "downloads," and he thought that the older gentleman would likely think that he was "a greedy Hollywood jerk, grubbing for yet more dough." Fortunately, the older gentleman smiled and introduced him to his wife, saying, "This is Bart Simpson! He wants more money from the computer! He's a good guy!" Mr. Long immediately thought, "God bless America, and God bless the Writers Guild."[179]

• Jack Klugman starred with Tony Randall in TV's *The Odd Couple*, and both actors made lots of money. Mr. Klugman never saw the money because it was sent directly to his business manager, but he decided that one week he wanted his money to be paid to himself in cash. On payday, a uniformed guard gave him a very large briefcase filled with $100 bills packed in bundles of $5,000. Mr. Klugman looked at the money and touched it. He then told the uniformed guard, "Take it back and have it sent to my business guy. I've seen it. I've touched it. Now I know it's real."[180]

• People whose job is creating funny cartoons tend to be funny. Tex Avery once lost $10 in a card game to his boss, Leon Schlesinger. He didn't have the money then, but paid it a little later: He walked into his boss' office with $10 in pennies, dumped the 1,000 pennies on his boss' desk, and walked out. Chuck Jones once owed Mr. Schlesinger $5: Mr. Jones paid it back with 500 pennies in a jar of honey. Benny Washam once owed $5 to Tedd Pierce and paid it back with 500 pennies baked inside a homemade loaf of bread.[181]

• As a high school student, comedian Jay Leno, host of *The Tonight Show*, worked at a McDonald's, where he says that he and his coworkers gave away free food. Some friends of Jay's would come in, order huge amounts of food, and Jay would say, "Ten burgers, eight fries, thirty shakes—that will be a quarter." The McDonald's manager once asked him, "We lost $25,000 last month. What happened?" Jay replied, "Oh, gosh, I must have given the last guy the wrong change."[182]

• As a young teenager, Oprah Winfrey disliked her eyeglasses, thinking that they made her look ugly. She asked her mother to buy her new eyeglasses, but money was hard to come by, and her mother said no. Therefore, when she was alone, Oprah wrecked the apartment and broke her eyeglasses, then said that "robbers" had broken into the apartment and done the damage. Her mother was forced to buy her new eyeglasses.[183]

• Many of the actors associated with *The Dick Van Dyke Show* signed a "six-play contract," which specified that they would be paid only for the first six times an episode was shown on TV, and after that they would receive nothing. Rose Marie, who played Sally Rogers, says, "Everybody thinks we're all still making money on the show. People think I'm filling mattresses with money—and I'm not!"[184]

• Charlie Chaplin was dissatisfied with the title of his movie *The Great Dictator*. He had wanted to simply call it *The Dictator*, but Paramount owned that title and Paramount wanted $25,000 to allow Mr. Chaplin to use it. Mr. Chaplin said, "I can't spend $25,000 for two words. So I said, 'All right, I'll call mine *The Great Dictator*—three words and all free.'"[185]

• Actress Diana Rigg appeared for two seasons on *The Avengers*. During the first year, she made £150 a week, but during the summer between the two seasons, she stated, "I'm worth at least three times that" and refused to come back to the series unless she got the money. The producers realized that she was right about her worth and paid her £450 a week.[186]

Mothers

• Some roles lead to more recognition than others. Danny Trejo, the star of Richard Rodriguez' *Machete* and a character actor who has appeared in hundreds of small roles, once told his mother that he had appeared in a movie with the great Robert De Niro. His mother was not impressed: "Oh, it's just play-acting—get a real job." But then for four days he played a character on the TV soap opera *The Young and the Restless*, and his mother was ecstatic: "Ah, mijo, you finally made it!" [187]

Music

• Joseph Barbera and William Hanna are famous for their Hanna-Barbera cartoons, featuring such stars as Yogi Berra, Huckleberry Hound, Tom and Jerry, and—of course—the Flintstones. Mr. Barbera was in an elevator with some people, including a lawyer wearing a buttoned-down collar. The lawyer began to hum *The Flintstones* theme song, and Mr. Barbera bet him $100 that he couldn't sing it all the way through. The lawyer sang it all the way through with gusto, and by the way the elevator had reached the lobby, everyone else in the elevator had joined in the singing. Mr. Barbera said, "It was the most satisfying hundred dollars I've ever spent—though I'm just as glad I hadn't offered a thousand."[188]

• Overweight actor John Banner played Sergeant Schultz, a German prisoner of war camp guard, in TV's *Hogan's Heroes*. In real life, he was a Jew and during World War II, he had been a sergeant in the United States Army. Back then, he was slim and even served as a model in a series of recruiting posters for the Army. By the way, Mr. Banner used to perform at state fairs with a rock and roll band while dressed in his Sergeant Schultz ("I know nothing! I see NOTHING!") uniform.[189]

Names

• Soupy Sales' real name was Milton Supman. His older brothers were nicknamed Hambone and Chickenbone, so Milton was nicknamed Soupbone, which later was shortened to Soupy. Later, he became known as Soupy Sales, at the suggestion of a Detroit TV station manager named John Pival, who remembered a funny comic actor who was named Chick Sale. This was fine with Soupy, and he became famous as Soupy Sales, but it did lead to one problem. He received a telephone call telling him that his children had not been attending school for weeks. This was a shock because his children had been attending school every day. It turned out that his children, Tony and Hunt Supman, had not been saying "present" when the name Supman was called because they thought that their last name was Sales. [190]

• Like other actors, Archibald Leach took a new name. He had played the role of a character named Cary Lockwood, so he took the name "Cary." He needed something shorter than "Lockwood" so it would easily fit on a movie marquee, so his movie studio produced its list of short Anglo-Saxon names that it kept on hand for actors with Archie's problem, and Mr. Leach read down the list, decided that he liked the name "Grant," and so he became Cary Grant.[191]

• Teenage mega-pop star Miley Cyrus was named Destiny Hope Cyrus at birth, but her always smiley face led to her being nicknamed first Smiley and then Miley. After becoming a huge star in Disney's *Hannah Montana* TV series, she had her name legally changed to Miley. Her father is country singer Billy Ray Cyrus, best known for "Achy Breaky Heart," and Miley has always been around music. Her first memory is of an all-star concert where superstars such as Aretha Franklin made a fuss over her.[192]

• In the 1960s TV series *Get Smart*, the audience never learns Agent 99's real name. At her wedding to Maxwell Smart, the audience could have learned it, but when the preacher pronounces her name, a loud snore from Max's best man, the elderly Admiral, drowns it out. [193]

• When Oprah Winfrey was born, her parents wanted to name her Orpah, after a person in the Book of Ruth. However, because of a misspelling on her birth certificate, she received the name that she later made famous.[194]

Parents

• Shortly after Kenneth Branagh's movie *Hamlet* came out, he and his parents met USA President Bill Clinton at a dinner. President Clinton told Mr. Branagh that he loved his movies, and Mr. Branagh looked at his parents, who seemed about to collapse. Mr., Branagh says, "And then when we went through the next door, my mother threw herself at Goldie Hawn and said, 'Do you know what the president just said to my son?'"[195]

People with Handicaps

• TV's Mister Rogers cared about his television neighbors. Part of his routine on his show was to feed the fish every day, but a blind child wrote in to ask if the fish were being fed because she couldn't see him feeding the fish. After reading the letter, Mister Rogers began to speak while feeding the fish to let her know that yes, the fish were being fed. [196]

Politics

• Margaret Thatcher was a formidable woman and a formidable politician, and her staff was afraid of her. Once, she held a meeting with her staff—yes-men all—and then they went to a restaurant for lunch. The waiter asked Mrs. Thatcher for her order, and she ordered beef. He then asked her, "And the vegetables?" Mrs. Thatcher replied, "They will have the beef as well." (Actually, this is a joke from a TV satirical puppet show titled *Spitting Image*.)[197]

• An episode of *Laugh-In* once showed Richard Nixon saying in a puzzled voice, "Sock it to me?" This may have lightened up his image enough to get a few votes from young voters and so become President of the United States. At least, some people thought that that was plausible. In fact, singer Lena Horne once kicked *Laugh-In* co-host Dick Martin and said, "You son of a bitch, you elected that bastard!" [198]

Practical Jokes

• Comedian Tim Conway served as producer-director of an Ohio TV program titled *Ernie's Place*, which featured Ernie Anderson. The program had no budget, and so each week Mr. Conway appeared as a guest on the show. One of the things that he and Mr. Anderson would do was to announce that a local notable such as the Mayor was going to appear on the show and be interviewed, but none of the local notables actually wanted to be on the show. When Mr. Conway and Mr. Anderson would announce that the Mayor was going to be on the show, the Mayor would telephone them and say that there was no way he would be on the show. But Mr. Conway and Mr. Anderson would announce on air that the Mayor had telephoned to say that he was on his way. They would keep teasing the audience like that until they would say that the Mayor had finally arrived, but it was too late to interview him. Because they did this so frequently, Mr. Conway says, "The audience soon got on to us." By the way, Mr. Conway married his own godmother. In 1958, he converted to Catholicism, and when the priest asked him who would serve as his godmother, Mr. Conway suggested the young woman he was dating. The priest advised against that because perhaps Mr. Conway and the young woman would get married and then Mr. Conway would be marrying his own godmother. So the priest suggested that Mary Anne Dalton, a friend of the couple, should be Mr. Conway's godmother. This suggestion was accepted, and she became Mr. Conway's godmother. However, he broke up with his girlfriend and started dating Ms. Dalton, and on May 27, 1961, he married his own godmother.[199]

• Not all practical jokes work out the way they are supposed to. When May Wale Brown was script supervisor on *Bonanza*, one of her jobs was to make sure that none of the actors wore a wristwatch during the filming as only pocket watches were used at the time the series was set. Dan Blocker, who played Hoss, was a big, gentle man who owned an expensive watch he was proud of. One day, as Ms. Brown was looking at all the actors' wrists to check for wristwatches, Mr. Blocker said, "I'm sick and tired of you telling me to take my watch off!" Then he threw his watch on the ground and stomped on it. Ms. Brown started crying, and Mr. Blocker told her, "You were supposed to tell me off—not cry!" The whole thing was an elaborate setup. Everyone but Ms. Brown knew about it, and Mr. Blocker had stomped on a cheap watch, not the expensive watch he was proud of. To make up for the practical joke that had backfired, Mr. Blocker bought Ms. Brown an expensive watch.[200]

• Australian actress Lisa Lackey's dream was to appear in her favorite TV series, *NYPD Blue*. In its final season, she managed to appear in one episode, during the filming of which director Mark Tinker played a joke on her. She acted in a courtroom scene in which she had lots of exposition, and Mr. Tinker said to her afterward, "Is that it? Is that the best you can do?" Ms. Lackey says, "Oh, my God, I nearly died. I think I almost wet my pants." What was also bad was that everybody on the set got quiet. Mr. Tinker then said, "I'm just kidding. That was great. Welcome to the family." Ms. Lackey jokes, "Oh, my God, I hate that man!" Of course, the experience of filming the episode was good, and Ms. Lackey says, "... what a fantastic cast of people. The best. That was the highlight of my career, I have to say." She also told a girlfriend, exaggerating a little, "This is it! I can give up now! I can go off and have a family and not worry about acting anymore!"[201]

• Carroll O'Meara was the producer of the radio show *The Phantom Pilot*. At the beginning of each episode, the announcer said, "The Phantom Pilot rides in Skyball!" This was followed by the sound of an airplane taking off. Once, the crew of *The Phantom Pilot* set the studio clocks ahead 10 minutes. Mr. O'Meara arrived at the studio and looked at the studio clock, then glanced at his watch, figured it was running slow, and called for action. As usual, the announcer said, "The Phantom Pilot rides in Skyball!" This time, however, during takeoff the sound effects man filled the room with sound of a terrific crash, and the announcer cried, "Oh, no! He didn't make it!" Mr. O'Meara's face went white, but his crew explained the joke, and a few minutes later the airplane took off as usual safely.[202]

• After Chuck Norris got married, he appeared on the Regis Philbin and Kathie Lee Gifford TV show *Live with Regis and Kathie Lee*, and with Regis' permission, he played a practical joke on Kathie Lee. Chuck told his hosts that he had played action heroes his entire career and that he wanted to be more romantic. He then asked if it would be OK for him to practice with someone from the audience. It was OK, and he chose a beautiful woman from the audience and kissed her passionately for a long time, shocking Kathie Lee. After the kiss, Chuck turned to Kathie Lee and said, "I'd like you to meet my wife, Gena."[203]

• Lee Greenway, a makeup man on *The Andy Griffith Show*, was a practical joker. An extra once came in for his makeup job at the beginning of the week, and Mr. Greenway asked him to remove his left shoe, then he put on the extra's makeup. The next day, the extra again came in for his makeup job, and Mr. Greenway said, "Forgot to take your shoe off." After the extra took off his left shoe, Mr. Greenway put on his makeup. The following day, the extra came in for his makeup job, and he started to take off his left shoe, but Mr. Greenway said, "No, no, this is Wednesday. We don't take our shoe off on Wednesday."[204]

• Ben Hecht and Charles MacArthur wrote the screenplay for *Wuthering Heights*, one of critic Alexander Woollcott's favorite books. Mr. Woollcott invited Mr. Hecht and Mr. MacArthur to his island, where he hoped to find out details of their screenplay. Knowing how snoopy Mr. Woollcott was, Mr. Hecht and Mr. MacArthur deliberately faked pages of their screenplay and left them out for Mr. Woollcott to find—the pages portrayed Heathcliff as a Wild West cowboy with sixshooters.[205]

• Sports announcer Phil Rizzuto had his own way of keeping a scorebook. He used "PO" for "pop out," "GO" for "ground out," and "FO" for "fly out". Once, he took a break, then came back to find that fellow announcer Joe Garagiola has written "WL" in his scorebook. He asked what "WL" meant, and Mr. Garagiola replied, "Wasn't looking." [206]

Chapter 5: From Problem-Solving to Work

Problem-Solving

• As a fashion designer for the movies, Edith Head had to be a problem-solver. For example, in 1965 Joan Crawford presented the Oscar for Best Director at the Academy Awards, and she asked Ms. Head to design her dress. One problem was that they did not know whether the actress presenting an Oscar before Ms. Crawford would be wearing black or white, so Ms. Head made two dresses: one black and one white. The other actress wore white, so Ms. Crawford put on the black dress. And Mae West liked to wear very tight dresses, so Ms. Head would make two versions of each dress for her: a very tight dress for Ms. West to wear during scenes in which she was standing up, and a slightly less tight dress for her to wear during scenes in which she was sitting down. A final example: Ms. Head designed sarongs for Dorothy Lamour to wear in movies. However, in the movie *Jungle Princess*, Ms. Lamour was in a pool of water when she suddenly screamed—and her sarong floated to the surface of the water. After that, instead of using knots that could come loose when wet, Ms. Head sewed Ms. Lamour into her sarong.[207]

• In 1944, Jerry Springer was born in a tube station in London, and five years later, his family took him to the United States. In New York City, when young Jerry attended his first day of class, he was dressed like a schoolboy in England: he wore knee socks, blue shorts, a jacket, a bow tie, and a beret. He remembers, "The kids beat the crap out of me, and they ripped my suit. And the second day, the same thing. Well, I'm running out of suits, and [my mom's] running out of sons." Fortunately, his mother was a problem-solver. She consulted a neighbor who told her that the schoolkids loved the Yankees, and so she bought Jerry a pinstriped Yankee uniform. Jerry says, "The kids in school loved it. ...

Every day to class in first and second grades I wore Yankee uniforms. I was afraid to go to school without it. That became my acceptance in America."[208]

• George Burns often read and gave advice about scripts for the TV sitcom *The People's Choice*. He was also a problem-solver. Sometimes, he read a script and realized that it had a problem. If he couldn't figure out what was wrong with the script, he would go to Hillcrest, a club that he and many other Hollywood people frequented. He then would start talking to a TV writer who made $250,000 a year and tell the writer the story in the script and say that it was a great story. The TV writer would look at him as if he were crazy and tell him what was wrong with the script. Then Mr. Burns would tell his partner in *The People's Choice* what was wrong with the script but not tell him how he had learned what was wrong with the script. Mr. Burns says that everyone thought that he was a genius.[209]

• *The Mary Tyler Moore Show*, a very popular TV sitcom of the 1970s, starred the popular actress as the much-beloved Mary Richards. When the show was filming its last episode, a problem arose. Sitcoms are supposed to be funny, and the cast and crew were weepy. Fortunately, a Western was being filmed nearby, so a producer brought in actors wearing Native American costumes to sit in chairs backstage as the actors rehearsed their scenes. At first, Ms. Moore was unaware of the actors backstage, but she was getting laughs in the wrong places, so she snuck a look—and laughed. The cast and crew were able to keep themselves from crying until the episode had been filmed.[210]

• When Matt Groening of *The Simpsons* and *Life in Hell* fame first went to Los Angeles after graduating from college, he lived in an apartment whose rent he could barely pay, and he had a neighbor downstairs who enjoyed playing his stereo at full volume. Mr. Groening tried various things to make the neighbor stop playing the stereo so loudly, including yelling, stomping his feet, and loudly playing his own stereo. All of these things were ineffective. Eventually, Mr. Groening was able to solve the problem by dropping a cinder block onto his floor. That got the downstairs tenant's attention, and the downstairs tenant turned down his stereo.[211]

• The hosts of TV entertainment news programs such as *Access Hollywood* need to be creative and think of ways to attract the attention of stars on the red carpet at such awards shows as the Emmys so that they can get a quick interview with them. Of course, interviews with normally reticent stars are especially prized. Nancy O'Dell, host of *Access Hollywood*, especially wanted an interview with multiple Oscar-winner Jack Nicholson. She thought about ways to get his attention on the red carpet, and finally she came with a winner: she wore a low-cut top.[212]

• In an episode of *The Many Loves of Dobie Gillis*, Maynard G. Krebs, played by Bob Denver, carried a box filled with bullfrogs. When he opened the box, the bullfrogs were supposed to jump out. However, during three takes, the bullfrogs did nothing but lie in the box. During the fourth take, the bullfrogs couldn't wait to jump out of the box. Mr. Denver knew that there had to be a trick involved, so he asked the propman how he had made the bullfrogs so active. The propman answered, "Tabasco sauce."[213]

• When Billy Wilder was directing *The Emperor Waltz* in 1948, he wanted a scene in which 250 women curtseyed for longer than a minute—something difficult to do in the heavy period costumes the actresses were wearing. In fact, while shooting the scene, one or more women would lose her balance and wobble or fall over. Mr. Wilder solved the problem by using very small stools fitted under each skirt so that the women could sit on them. Then he was able to film the curtsy in only one take.[214]

• Actress Greta Garbo liked wearing pants. Once, she wanted to dine at a particular LA restaurant that forbade pants for women. She simply rolled up her pants so that her coat would hide them, then she dined there. While filming her movies, she wore furry bedroom slippers when her feet would not be shown on screen, and she often asked her cameraman, "Is the feets in?"[215]

• Sarah Michelle Gellar of *Buffy the Vampire Slayer* TV fame once had a problem. She was dressed fabulously because she was going to the Blockbuster Movie Awards, but unfortunately she was having her driveway refinished and couldn't figure out how to get to her car without ruining her outfit. Fortunately, the workers in her driveway knew exactly what to do to solve the problem—they carried her to her car.[216]

• Nicholas Brendan played Xander in the TV cult series *Buffy the Vampire Slayer*. Of course, very quickly he became famous and he was often recognized in the streets. Kelly, his twin brother, got so tired of being mistaken for Nicholas that he dyed his hair blond.[217]

• Is it possible to have a tap-dancing show on the radio? Yes. Fred Astaire used to tap dance on the radio—he danced on a small box made of oak, which is commonly used on dance floors. The radio audience listened to the sound of his dancing.[218]

Public Speaking

• Orson Welles was multi-talented, although multi-geniused might be a better adjective. He spent a lot of time doing things to make money so that he could make his own independent films, and many people think that some of the things he worked on were not worthy of his genius. Sometimes, late in his life, he gave lectures in middle America to audiences that did not fill all of the seats available. He would introduce himself, correctly, as a film director, an actor, a writer, a painter, a designer, and a magician, and then he would scan the audience and say, "Isn't it strange that there are so many of me and so few of you?"[219]

Quiz Shows

• On Groucho Marx' *You Bet Your Life* TV quiz show, a man appeared who claimed to be an Arab prince. Groucho grew suspicious after a while, and he discovered that the man was actually Bill Blatty, a writer whose mother was Arab. Mr. Blatty often pretended to be an Arab prince at parties. Groucho asked him, "Are you a wolf in sheep's clothing?" Mr. Blatty replied, "In sheikh's clothing." Mr. Blatty was clever enough to win (with his partner) $10,000. When Groucho asked what he would do with his share of the money, Mr. Blatty replied, "It's going to finance me to finish my book." The money did exactly that. Bill Blatty was William Peter Blatty, and the book was the novel *The Exorcist*.[220]

• A priest who guested on Groucho Marx's quiz show *You Bet Your Life* told him, "I want to thank you for all the joy you've put into the world." Groucho replied, "And I want to thank you for all the joy you've taken out of it."[221]

Romance

• The episode of *The Mary Tyler Moore Show* titled "Lou Dates Mary" should be titled "Mary Dates Lou" because in it, Mary Richards asks Lou Grant for a date. The episode shows that Mr. Grant is sensitive—he can't remember Mary's favorite flower so he brings her three different bouquets—and a bag of nuts.[222]

Satire

• In the satiric movie *Idiocracy*, two average people from our time go into the future, where they are geniuses in comparison with the people living then because the culture has been dumbed down so much. However, in December 2011 movie critic Jim Emerson's mother had an interesting experience trying to pay her cable bill in person. First, the background. Jim Emerson's father had died, and two years later, the cable company closed his account (which his mother had been paying). The cable company opened a new account for her. She sent in the cable TV payment, and the cable company applied it to the old account, not her new account. This made her new account past due. She contacted the cable company, which offered to send her a refund check that would arrive in a few weeks, but the cable company wanted her to make the payment on the new account. She did this, and guess what—the cable company credited this payment to the old account! She decided to go to the cable company in person and make the payment on her new account. The amount "owed" was $114.25, and she gave the cashier $120 in bills, intending of course to get $5.75 in change back. The cashier said that he did not have 75 cents in coins to give her as part of her change, so she gave him a quarter so that she would get $6 in change back. The casher said again that he didn't have any coins. She pointed out that she had just given him a quarter so now the change owed her was $6, not $5.75. The cashier said again that he didn't have 75 cents. Finally, Jim Emerson's mother gifted the cable company the 75 cents. Apparently, satire can't keep up with reality.[223]

Screenwriters

• Jules Feiffer wrote the screenplay for the movie *Popeye*, which was supposed to star Dustin Hoffman in the title role. Mr. Hoffman decided not to act in the movie, however, thus upsetting Mr. Feiffer, who picked up a script that Mr. Hoffman did like. Mr. Feiffer yelled, "You make me jump through hoops to find out why you won't do my beautiful screenplay, and instead you're going to do *this*?" The script was for the movie *Kramer Versus Kramer*, for which Mr. Hoffman won a Best Actor Oscar.[224]

Sitcoms

• Actress Suzanne Pleshette is best known for her role as the TV wife of Bob Hartley, played by comedian Bob Newhart, on the hit sitcom *The Bob Newhart Show*. As Emily Hartley, she was pretty and sexy and memorable; however, her funniest TV moment may have come at the very end of another series starring Mr. Newhart: the series titled *Newhart*, in which his character runs a country inn in Vermont. At the end of the series finale, Bob wakes up in bed next to Emily, and the audience learns that the entire series *Newhart* was actually a dream caused by Bob Hartley's eating too much Japanese food before going to bed. This, of course, became a part of pop culture, and the satiric *Onion* once ran a 1999 story with the headline "Universe Ends as God Wakes

Up Next to Suzanne Pleshette." Ms. Pleshette was known for her deep, smoky voice. She once said, "Telephone operators have called me 'sir' since I was 6."[225]

• British comedian Omid Djalili's family came from Iran, and he has appeared in much media, including Whoopi Goldberg's 2003-2004 NBC sitcom, in which he played a handyman. Ms. Goldberg wanted him to have good and funny lines, and she got on one of her writers about it. Mr. Djalili says, "She told the scriptwriter, 'We have someone who's a Perrier-nominated comedian [the Perrier comedy awards, now known as the if.comedy awards, are given to the best comedy shows at the Edinburgh Festival Fringe] and all you can write for him are Ayatollah jokes. Is that all he's good for? It's my show. Write him some proper sh*t.'"[226]

• Lucille Ball was clearly the star of *I Love Lucy*, and everybody knew it, including her husband and co-star Desi Arnazi and including Jess Oppenheimer, who came up with the concept of the show. Occasionally, creative differences came up between these three people, and Desi proposed that the differences be decided by majority rule: if Lucy and Desi disagreed with Jess, then Lucy and Desi would get their way, and if Lucy and Jess disagreed with Desi, then Lucy and Jess would get their way. Jess asked what would happen when Desi and Jess agreed. Desi replied, "Like I told you, majority rules. In that case, then Lucy decides."[227]

Sports

• Actor and musician Tim Robbins, who won a Best Supporting Actor Oscar in 2003 for *Mystic River*, is a sports fan. On his 11st birthday, he and his grandmother sat in the last row of Shea Stadium as the New York Mets won the World Series. The fans went onto the field and grabbed handfuls of grass as souvenirs. Tim remembers, "I really wanted to join this madness on the subway, but I could see the terror in my grandmother's eyes. On the way home a guy gave me some of his big wad of grass. I kept it for years." He also plays hockey, and he says, "Ice hockey is a really cerebral game. It can be a beautiful ballet. But I have to keep my head up when I am playing as there's always that *sshole who recognizes you and wants to tell their friends how they laid Tim Robbins out on the ice."[228]

Telegrams

• Red Skelton was a talented comedian, but even talented comedians need writers. Jack Douglas was a professional writer for radio comedians, including Bob Hope. He heard an early episode of *The Red Skelton Show* on the radio and was so appalled by the show's comic material that he sent Red this telegram: "DEAR RED, I HEARD YOUR SHOW LAST NIGHT. YOU NEED ME. JACK DOUGLAS." Jack got a job and wrote comic material for Mr. Skelton for years.[229]

Telephones

• Dick Wolf, executive producer of *Law & Order* and all of its spinoffs, occasionally has to make tough decisions. NBC's President of Entertainment Warren Littlefield called him when *Law & Order* was in its fourth season. Mr. Wolf remembers, "Warren called up and said, 'You've got to put women in the show.' And I said, 'Well, I just can't add characters. That means I'd have to make some changes.' He said, 'Exactly.'" Mr. Wolf added S. Epatha Merkerson and Jill Hennessy to the cast, but that meant that he had to fire two male members of the cast. One of those two was Dann Florek. Mr. Wolf called Mr. Florek and told him, "Look, you know, this is a very difficult call. You're the guy who's first there every day. You always know your lines. You never bump into the furniture. You're fired.' It was terrible. It was the worst call of my professional career." Fortunately, Mr. Florek later was rehired to play the captain on *Law & Order: Special Victims Unit*.[230]

Thanksgiving

• Kitty Carlisle Hart, a panelist on the TV show *To Tell the Truth*, was not a cook, but once she agreed to cook Thanksgiving supper for her family during a trip. This meant that the family cook would do all the real work of prepping the food. All Ms. Hart would have to do was such things as popping the turkey in the oven, turning on the stove, and waiting the required amount of time. All seemed to be going well, but when she checked on the food, the vegetables and gravy were fine, but she discovered that she had forgotten to turn on the stove, so the turkey was raw. The Hart family ate Thanksgiving supper at a Howard Johnson's, and they decided to tell their cook, Alma, that her turkey was the best that they had ever had.[231]

• Len Evans, a publicist for Project Publicity, came out to his mother on a Thanksgiving Eve. He and his mother were watching an episode of *Will and Grace* in which the gay character Jack is trying to hide his gayness from his mother, and his friends Grace and Karen are pretending to be his girlfriends. Len's mother turned to him and said, "This show reminds me of you and your friends. Is there something you want to tell me?" He then admitted that he was gay. He says, "She hugged me and said she had been waiting for me to tell her for years. I guess it's true that a mother always knows...."[232]

Valentine's Day

• Even celebrities had (and have) bad days, weeks, and more. When Canadian actress Neve Campbell was nine years old, her elementary class had a Valentine's Day during which students could buy a cookie for a nickel and gave it to a classmate. The teacher would call the student to the front of the class, and the student would get the cookie and the name of the friend who had bought it for them. On this horrible Valentine's Day, Neve's name was called only once — for a cookie that her *teacher* had bought her. Neve says, "I was devastated. No one would spend five cents to send me a cookie." Later, while she was attending the National Ballet School, her unpopularity continued. The male dancers wrote a song that listed all the girls from prettiest to ugliest. The last verse — which went, "Neve-aagh! Neve-aagh!" — revealed that the boys thought that Neve was the ugliest girl in class. Of course, Neve turned out pretty well. Few, if any, people think that the co-star of the TV series *Party of Five* and the movie *Wild Things* is anything other than beautiful.[233]

Wit

• On *You Bet Your Life*, Groucho Marx asked a beautiful model what her most exciting experience had been, but she couldn't remember any. Groucho commented, "A model with no exciting memories? What were you modeling—clay?" On another episode, a very pretty and very shapely tennis player told Groucho that she was working on her form. Groucho eyed her, then said, "If your form improves, you are going to need all the speed you can muster."[234]

Work

• Cartoon director Chuck Jones worked on a cartoon starring Marc Anthony, a bulldog who adopts a kitten. The only dialogue is by a woman, and so expressions are incredibly important. At one point, the woman says to Marc Anthony, "What are you up to now?" Marc Anthony points to himself and assumes an expression of exaggerated innocence. Mr. Jones worked hard to get that expression right. He created and rejected a minimum of 50 drawings before he got the expression exactly right. He remembered, "I needed *that* drawing, and I knew it was somewhere between my memory and the tip of my pencil, but there was a sort of cornucopia of unsuitable drawings before I finally got the right one. Mr. Jones told a parable about a Japanese painter whom a rich man commissioned to create a painting of a stork for $10,000. The painting was supposed to be done in two months, but at that time the Japanese painter told the rich man to come back in another two months. When the rich man came back after waiting for four months, the Japanese painter took out his paints and created the painting of a stork in ten minutes. The rich man thought that he had been cheated: "Ten thousand dollars for that? It took you no longer than ten minutes!" The Japanese painter opened a cabinet door and thousands of drawings of storks fell out. Mr. Jones stated, "I didn't do a thousand drawings of Marc Anthony's look of exaggerated innocence, but I did do at least fifty before I got it right, and that doesn't count the thousands of drawings I had done when I was learning to draw this dog, after learning how to draw *any* dog, after learning how to draw." [235]

• Benny Washam wanted to work in animation, and he became an in-betweener for Leon Schlesinger. He started out making $6 a week. Within a month, his salary was raised to $12 a week. In 1936, at the end of his first year, he was making $25 a month. Thereafter, he often went into Mr. Schlesinger's office to ask for a raise, but Mr. Schlesinger always asked, "Are you better than Ken Harris?" (Mr. Harris was another animator at the studio.) Mr. Washam was forced to answer, "No." Mr. Schlesinger would then say, "Ken's always satisfied with what he's getting." After a year of asking for raises and getting turned down, Mr. Washam walked into Mr. Schlesinger's office and said, "I demand a raise for Ken Harris!" By the way, Mr. Harris really loved animation. In the early 1930s, the time of the Great Depression, he even paid $10 a week—a lot of money at the time—so he could work as an animator. After six months of paying $10 a week, Mr. Harris got good news. The studio felt that he could become one of the top animators in the world, and so his boss wanted to give him a raise: Mr. Harris could work for him for nothing—he no longer had to pay him $10 a week![236]

• Sometimes, you need the courage to stand up for your beliefs. When Mel Brooks was a comedy writer for Sid Caesar, Mr. Brooks wrote a sketch featuring Mr. Caesar as a German professor, but Mr. Caesar did not want to do it. As they walked together on the street, Mr. Caesar kept saying, "No," as Mr. Brooks tried to convince him to do the sketch. Finally, out of frustration, Mr. Brooks, who is a small man, hit Mr. Caesar, who is a big man, in the face. Mr. Caesar looked at Mr. Brooks and said, "I'll let you live." However, Mr. Caesar was impressed that Mr. Brooks believed so strongly in the sketch, so he did it on TV and discovered that Mr. Brooks was correct about the funniness of the

German professor and the sketch. Thereafter, Mr. Caesar appeared on his TV show as the German professor many times.[237]

• Character actor Jay Thomas played Eddie LeBec, the boyfriend of Carla Tortelli, who was played by Rhea Perlman, on *Cheers*. Mr. Thomas also hosted a popular morning radio show in Los Angeles, California. Of course, his portrayal of Mr. LeBec brought him a lot of attention, and someone called in to the radio show to ask him about what it was like to appear on *Cheers* in a recurring role. According to *Cheers* writer Ken Levine, "He said something to the effect of, 'It's brutal. I have to kiss Rhea Perlman.' Well, guess who happened to be listening ... Jay Thomas was never seen on *Cheers* again."[238]

• Danny Trejo, the star of Richard Rodriguez' *Machete*, works—a lot. He appears in film after film. For example, he made the high-profile movie *Machete* at roughly the same time he appeared in a movie titled *Blacktino*—for which he made $100. This isn't necessarily a sign of a need to work constantly. Instead, he says, "I like to do as many student films and [work with as many] first-time directors as I can." His kids are getting involved with making movies as well. His son Gilbert is producing a movie titled *Skinny-Dip*, and Danny jokes, "He better hire me. I don't want to hear, 'Dad, you're too old for the part.'"[239]

• When she was studying to be an actress in Chicago, Virginia Madsen worked as a waitress at P.S. Chicago. When a movie company was shooting *Class*, she got a small role in which she played one of the students at the school. One day, she was acting in a scene and during a break she saw her manager from P.S. Chicago. Virginia asked her manager if she was an extra in the movie. The manager replied that she was not, and then she asked Virginia a question: "Aren't you supposed to be at P.S. Chicago right now working as a waitress?"[240]

• Not every job interview goes the way we want it to. As a young man wanting to break into publishing, Garrison Keillor, now of *A Prairie Home Companion* fame, took a bus to Boston for an interview for a job at *The Atlantic*. He arrived an hour early, went to a bathroom in the *Atlantic* building, took off his shirt and washed himself with paper towels. During this bathing process, a man came into the bathroom and made an effort not to look at him. As you may expect, given the world we live in, this man turned out to be the man interviewing Mr. Keillor, who says, "It was a polite interview and I did not get the job."[241]

• When actor Brian Blessed was performing in the British TV series *Z-Cars*, he worked for director Herbie Wise, who would fire people immediately if he felt that they needed to be fired. Once, Mr. Blessed arrived for work eight hours late and said, with tears in his eyes, that his mother had died. This excuse worked, and so he used it at other times when he needed a good excuse. He stopped when his mother telephoned him and requested, "Brian, would you stop killing me?" [242]

• Veronica Lake was a film siren of the 1940s—the era of Rosie the Riveter. She was famous for a hairstyle in which her tresses fell over one eye, leaving only one eye for her to use to see. According to legend, the United States government asked her to change her hairstyle because it was afraid that many industrial accidents would occur because so many Rosie the Riveters were imitating her hairstyle, thereby partially obscuring their vision.[243]

• Oral historian Studs Terkel had a show called *Stud's Place* in the early days of television, but he was blacklisted because—always interested in politics and the common man—he had signed many, many leftwing petitions. Someone asked him about the petitions, "Don't you know communists are behind this?" Mr. Terkel replied, "And if the communists are against cancer does that mean we have to be for cancer?"[244]

• Like many stars, Kristen Wiig, co-writer and lead of *Bridesmaids*, worked a series of ordinary jobs before becoming famous. Among those jobs was working as a waitress at Universal Studios. Sometimes, she will run into someone while she is working on a movie or a TV show, and she will wonder from where she knows that person: "And then I'll remember: Oh yeah, I used to serve you Cobb salad."[245]

• Rod Serling found becoming a published author difficult. Early in his career, the magazines he submitted his work to sent him forty rejection slips in a row. However, once he began to become successful, his workload on such projects as *The Twilight Zone* became enormous, and he smoked as much as four packs of cigarettes a day to help stimulate him enough to keep up with it.[246]

• Animated films, even short ones, can take years to complete. Nick Park, creator of Wallace and Gromit, paid actor Peter Sallis to do voice work (he is the voice of Wallace) on the half-hour animated film *A Grand Day Out*. Mr. Park says, "Seven years later, I phoned to tell him I had finally made the film, and he had no idea who I was."[247]

• Despite being a media celebrity, central Ohio sportscaster Jimmy Crum avoided getting a big head, perhaps because of the way he was treated when he first started in television. His right ear sticks out farther than his left ear, so his first station manager forced Mr. Crum to glue the ear to his head with chewing gum.[248]

• Early in his career, comedian Don Knotts hoped to get a job on *The Jackie Gleason Show*. He called the show's casting office and explained that he was a comedian and that he wanted to be on the show, but a voice—not Mr. Gleason's—told him, "We got a comedian," and then hung up.[249]

• Oprah Winfrey became the first black co-anchor and the first woman co-anchor in Nashville after she auditioned for WTVF-TV. She knew that her race and sex had helped her to get the job, but she says, "Sure, I was a token. But, honey, I was one happy token."[250]

Bonus Anecdote
• Jack Paar once walked off the set of *The Tonight Show* because the network censored one of his jokes. Three weeks later, he returned and said, "As I was saying before I was interrupted ...."[251]

APPENDIX A: BIBLIOGRAPHY

Adair, Gene. *Alfred Hitchcock: Filming Our Fears*. Oxford, England: Oxford University Press, 2002.

Adir, Karen. *The Great Clowns of American Television*. Jefferson, NC: McFarland & Company, Inc., 1988.

Adler, Bill. *Jewish Wit and Wisdom*. New York: Dell Publishing Co., Inc, 1969.

Adler, Bill, and Bruce Cassiday. *The World of Jay Leno: His Humor and His Life*. New York: Carol Publishing Group, 1992.

Aronson, Virginia. *Jennifer Love Hewitt*. Philadelphia, PA: Chelsea House Publishers, 2000.

Aucoin, Kevyn. Face*Forward*. Boston, MA: Little, Brown and Company, 2000.

Backus, Jim and Henny. *Forgive Us Our Digressions*. New York: St. Martin's Press, 1988.

Barbera, Joseph. *My Life in 'toons: From Flatbush to Bedrock in Under a Century*. Atlanta, Georgia: Turner Publishing, Inc., 1994.

Blanc, Mel, and Philip Bashe. *That's Not All, Folks*. New York: Warner Books, 1998.

Bogdanovich, Peter. *Peter Bogdanovich's Movie of the Week*. New York: Ballantine Books, 1999.

Bonner, Mike. *Jennifer Aniston*. Philadelphia, PA: Chelsea House Publishers, 2002.

Briggs, Joe Bob. *Profoundly Disturbing: Shocking Movies That Changed History!* New York: Universe Books, 2003.

Brown, David. *Star Billing: Tell-Tale Trivia from Hollywood*. London: Weidenfeld and Nicolson Limited, 1985.

Brown, May Wale. *Reel Life on Hollywood Movie Sets*. Riverside, CA: Ariadne Press, 1995.

Cavett, Dick. *Talk Show: Confrontations, Pointed Commentary, and Off-Screen Secrets*. New York: Henry Holt and Company, 2010.

Couric, Katie. *The Best Advice I Ever Got: Lessons from Extraordinary Lives*. New York: Random House, 2011.

Crum, Jimmy, and Carole Gerber. *How About That! Jimmy Crum: Fifty Years of Cliffhangers and Barn-Burners*. Columbus, OH: Fine Line Graphics, 1993.

Diamond, Kerry. *Kevyn Aucoin: A Beautiful Life*. New York: Atria Books, 2003.

Dougherty, Terri. *Ashton Kutcher*. Farmington Hills, MI: Lucent Books, 2007.

Edelsen, Edward. *Tough Guys and Gals of the Movies*. Garden City, NY: Doubleday and Co., Inc., 1978.

Edwards, Susan. *Erma Bombeck: A Life in Humor*. New York: Avon Books, 1997.

Epstein, Lawrence J. *George Burns: An American Life*. Jefferson, NC, and London: McFarland & Company, Inc., Publishers, 2011.

Farr, Jamie. *Just Farr Fun*. With Robert Blair Kaiser. Clearwater, Florida: Eubanks / Donizetti Inc., 1994.

Feldon, Barbara. *Living Alone and Loving It*. New York: Simon and Schuster, Inc., 2003.

Finn, Margaret L. *Mary Tyler Moore*. Philadelphia, PA: Chelsea House Publishers, 1997.

Fox, Patty. *Star Style: Hollywood Legends as Fashion Icons*. Santa Monica, CA: Angel City Press, Inc., 1995.

Franklin, Joe. *Up Late with Joe Franklin*. New York: Scribner, 1995.

Furniss, Maureen, editor. *Chuck Jones Conversations*. With the assistance of Stormy Gunter. Jackson, Mississippi: University Press of Mississippi, 2005.

Garagiola, Joe. *It's Anybody's Ballgame*. New York: Jove Books, 1988.

Garner, Joe. *Made You Laugh: the Funniest Moments in Radio, Television, Stand-up, and Movie Comedy*. Kansas City, MO: Andrews McMeel Publishing, 2004.

Golden, Christopher, and Nancy Holder. *Buffy the Vampire Slayer: The Watcher's Guide*. With Keith R.A. DeCandido. New York: Pocket Books, 1998.

Green, Amy Boothe, and Howard E. Green. *Remembering Walt: Favorite Memories of Walt Disney*. New York: Disney Editions, 1999.

Green, Joey. *The Get Smart Handbook*. New York: Collier Books, 1993.

Grobel, Lawrence. *Above the Line: Conversations About the Movies*. N.p.: Da Capo Press, 2000.

Grodin, Charles, et al. *If I Only Knew Then ... Learning from Our Mistakes*. New York: Springboard Press, 2007.

Guzmán, Lila and Rick. *George Lopez: Latino King*. Berkeley Heights, NJ: Enslow Publishers, Inc., 2009.

Hanna, Bill. *A Cast of Friends*. With Tom Ito. New York: Da Capo Press, 1996.

Harmon, Jim. *The Great Radio Heroes*. Jefferson, NC, and London: McFarland and Company, Inc., Publishers, 2001.

Hayes, Kevin J., editor. *Charlie Chaplin: Interviews*. Jackson, MS: University Press of Mississippi, 2005.

Head, Edith, and Paddy Calistro. *Edith Head's Hollywood*. New York: E.P. Dutton, Inc., 1983.

Hollingsworth, Amy. *The Simple Faith of Mister Rogers*. Nashville, TN: Integrity Publishers, 2005.

Jones, Chuck. *Chuck Amok: The Life and Times of an Animated Cartoonist*. New York: Farrar Straus Giroux, 1990.

Jones, Chuck. *Chuck Redux: Drawing from the Fun Side of Life*. New York: Warner Books, Inc. 1996.

Kanner, Bernice. *The 100 Best TV Commercials ... and Why They Worked*. New York: Times Books, 1999.

Kelly, Richard. *The Andy Griffith Show*. Winston-Salem, N.C.: John F. Blair, Publisher, 1981.

Kettelkamp, Larry. *Bill Cosby: Family Funny Man*. New York: Julian Messner, 1987.

Knotts, Don. *Barney Fife and Other Characters I Have Known*. With Robert Metz. New York: Berkley Boulevard Books, 1999.

Kohen, Yael. *We Killed: The Rise of Women in American Comedy*. New York: Farrar, Straus and Giroux, 2012.

Laslo, Cynthia. *Sarah Michelle Gellar*. New York: Children's Press, 2005.

Lemmon, Chris. *A Twist of Lemmon: A Tribute to My Father*. Chapel Hill, NC: Algonquin Books of Chapel Hill, 2006.

Loos, Anita. *Kiss Hollywood Goodbye*. New York: Ballantine Books, 1974.

Lutz, Norma Jean. *Britney Spears*. Philadelphia, PA: Chelsea House Publishers, 2000.

Lyman, Darryl. *The Jewish Comedy Catalog*. Middle Village, NY: Jonathan David Publishers, Inc., 1989.

Madison, Bob. *American Horror Writers*. Berkeley Heights, NJ: Enslow Publications, Inc., 2001.

Malone, Mary. *Connie Chung: Broadcast Journalist*. Hillside, NJ: Enslow Publishers, Inc., 1992.

Marx, Arthur. *Red Skelton*. New York: E.P. Dutton, 1979.

Marx, Groucho. *The Secret Word is Groucho*. With Hector Arce. New York: G.P. Putnam's Sons, 1976.

Mason, Paul. *Sarah Michelle Gellar*. Chicago, IL: Raintree, 2005.

McMahon, Ed. *For Laughing Out Loud: My Life and Good Times*. With David Fisher. New York: Warner Books, Inc., 1998.

McMahon, Ed. *Here's Johnny! My Memories of Johnny Carson, The Tonight Show, and 46 Years of Friendship*. Nashville, TN: Rutledge Hill Press, 2005.

Miller, Raymond H. *Matt Groening*. Farmington Hills, MI: KidHaven Press, 2006.

Michael Moore, *Here Comes Trouble: Stories from my Life*. New York: Hachette Book Group, 2011.

Nachman, Gerald. *Seriously Funny: The Rebel Comedians of the 1950s and 1960s*. New York: Pantheon Books, 2003.

Neuwirth, Allan. *They'll Never Put That on the Air: An Oral History of Taboo-Breaking TV Comedy*. New York: Allworth Press, 2006.

Norris, Chuck. *The Official Chuck Norris Fact Book*. With Todd DuBord. Carol Stream, IL: Tyndale House Publishers, Inc., Publishers, 2009.

Parla, Paul, and Charles P. Mitchell. *Screen Sirens Scream!* Jefferson, NC, and London: McFarland and Company, Inc., Publishers, 2000.

Pegg, Robert. *Comical Co-Stars of Television*. Jefferson, NC: McFarland & Company, Inc., Publishers, 2002.

Primack, Ben, adapter and editor. *The Ben Hecht Show: Impolitic Observations from the Freest Thinker of 1950s Television*. Jefferson, NC: McFarland & Company, Inc., Publishers, 1993.

Reisfeld, Randi, and Marie Morreale. *Got Issues Much: Celebrities Share Their Traumas and Triumphs*. New York: Scholastic Inc., 1999.

Rogers, Dave. *The Avengers*. London: Independent Television Books, Ltd., 1983.

Rogers, Fred. *You Are Special*. New York: Viking, 1994.

Royce, Brenda Scott. *Hogan's Heroes*. Jefferson, NC: McFarland & Company, Inc., Publishers, 1993.

Saidman, Anne. *Oprah Winfrey: Media Success Story*. Minneapolis, MN: Lerner Publications Company, 1990.

Sales, Soupy. *Soupy Sez! My Zany Life and Times*. With Charles Salzberg. New York: M. Evans and Company, Inc., 2001.

Sanford, Herb. *Ladies and Gentlemen, The Garry Moore Show: Behind the Scenes When TV was New*. New York: Stein and Day, Publishers, 1976.

Schafer, Kermit. *All Time Great Bloopers*. New York: Avenel Books, 1973.

Schafer, Kermit. *The Bedside Book of Celebrity Bloopers*. New York: Crown Publishers, Inc., 1984.

Schickel, Richard. *Cary Grant: A Celebration*. Boston, MA: Little, Brown and Company, 1983.

Schochet, Stephen. *Hollywood Stories: Short, Entertaining Anecdotes About the Stars and Legends of the Movies!* Los Angeles, CA: Hollywood Stories Publishing, 2010.

Sigall, Martha. *Living Life Inside the Lines: Tales from the Golden Age of Animation*. Jackson, Mississippi: University Press of Mississippi, 2005.

Smith, Ron. *Comic Support*. New York: Carol Publishing Group, 1993.

Stefoff, Rebecca. *Mary Tyler Moore: The Woman Behind the Smile*. New York: New American Library, 1986.

Taylor, Glenhall. *Before Television: The Radio Years*. New York: A.S. Barnes and Company, 1979.

Thomas, Marlo. *Growing Up Laughing: My Story and the Story of Funny*. Waterville, ME: Thorndike Press, 2010. Large Print.

Waldron, Vince. *Classic Sitcoms: A Celebration of the Best in Prime-Time Comedy*. New York: Macmillan Publishing Company, 1987.

Weissman, Ginny, and Coyne Steven Sanders. *The Dick Van Dyke Show*. New York: St. Martin's Press, 1993.

Wooten, Sara McIntosh. *Oprah Winfrey: Talk Show Legend*. Berkeley Heights, NJ: Enslow Publications, Inc., 1999.

Zoglin, Richard. *Comedy at the Edge: How Stand-up in the 1970s Changed America*. New York: Bloomsbury, 2008.

APPENDIX B: ABOUT THE AUTHOR

It was a dark and stormy night. Suddenly a cry rang out, and on a hot summer night in 1954, Josephine, wife of Carl Bruce, gave birth to a boy — me. Unfortunately, this young married couple allowed Reuben Saturday, Josephine's brother, to name their first-born. Reuben, aka "The Joker," decided that Bruce was a nice name, so he decided to name me Bruce Bruce. I have gone by my middle name — David — ever since.

Being named Bruce David Bruce hasn't been all bad. Bank tellers remember me very quickly, so I don't often have to show an ID. It can be fun in charades, also. When I was a counselor as a teenager at Camp Echoing Hills in Warsaw, Ohio, a fellow counselor gave the signs for "sounds like" and "two words," then she pointed to a bruise on her leg twice. Bruise Bruise? Oh yeah, Bruce Bruce is the answer!

Uncle Reuben, by the way, gave me a haircut when I was in kindergarten. He cut my hair short and shaved a small bald spot on the back of my head. My mother wouldn't let me go to school until the bald spot grew out again.

Of all my brothers and sisters (six in all), I am the only transplant to Athens, Ohio. I was born in Newark, Ohio, and have lived all around Southeastern Ohio. However, I moved to Athens to go to Ohio University and have never left.

At Ohio U, I never could make up my mind whether to major in English or Philosophy, so I got a bachelor's degree with a double major in both areas, then I added a master's degree in English and a master's degree in Philosophy.

Currently, and for a long time to come (I eat fruits and veggies), I am spending my retirement writing books such as *Nadia Comaneci: Perfect 10*, *The Funniest People in Dance*, *Homer's* Iliad: *A Retelling in Prose*, and *William Shakespeare's* Othello: *A Retelling in Prose*.

By the way, my sister Brenda Kennedy writes romances such as *A New Beginning* and *Shattered Dreams*.

APPENDIX C: SOME BOOKS BY DAVID BRUCE

Anecdote Books

250 Anecdotes About Opera

250 Anecdotes About Religion

250 Anecdotes About Religion: Volume 2

The Coolest People in Art: 250 Anecdotes

The Coolest People in Books: 250 Anecdotes

The Coolest People in Comedy: 250 Anecdotes

Don't Fear the Reaper: 250 Anecdotes

The Funniest People in Art: 250 Anecdotes

The Funniest People in Books: 250 Anecdotes

The Funniest People in Books, Volume 2: 250 Anecdotes

The Funniest People in Books, Volume 3: 250 Anecdotes

The Funniest People in Comedy: 250 Anecdotes

The Funniest People in Dance: 250 Anecdotes

The Funniest People in Families: 250 Anecdotes

The Funniest People in Families, Volume 2: 250 Anecdotes

The Funniest People in Families, Volume 3: 250 Anecdotes

The Funniest People in Families, Volume 4: 250 Anecdotes

The Funniest People in Families, Volume 5: 250 Anecdotes

The Funniest People in Families, Volume 6: 250 Anecdotes

The Funniest People in Movies: 250 Anecdotes

The Funniest People in Music: 250 Anecdotes

The Funniest People in Music, Volume 2: 250 Anecdotes

The Funniest People in Music, Volume 3: 250 Anecdotes

The Funniest People in Neighborhoods: 250 Anecdotes

The Funniest People in Relationships: 250 Anecdotes

The Funniest People in Sports: 250 Anecdotes

The Funniest People in Sports, Volume 2: 250 Anecdotes

The Funniest People in Television and Radio: 250 Anecdotes
The Funniest People in Theater: 250 Anecdotes
The Funniest People Who Live Life: 250 Anecdotes
The Funniest People Who Live Life, Volume 2: 250 Anecdotes
The Kindest People Who Do Good Deeds, Volume 1: 250 Anecdotes
The Kindest People Who Do Good Deeds, Volume 2: 250 Anecdotes
Maximum Cool: 250 Anecdotes
The Most Interesting People in Movies: 250 Anecdotes
The Most Interesting People in Politics and History: 250 Anecdotes
The Most Interesting People in Politics and History, Volume 2: 250 Anecdotes
The Most Interesting People in Politics and History, Volume 3: 250 Anecdotes
The Most Interesting People in Religion: 250 Anecdotes
The Most Interesting People in Sports: 250 Anecdotes
The Most Interesting People Who Live Life: 250 Anecdotes
The Most Interesting People Who Live Life, Volume 2: 250 Anecdotes
Resist Psychic Death: 250 Anecdotes
Seize the Day: 250 Anecdotes and Stories

Children's Biography

Nadia Comaneci: Perfect Ten

Discussion Guides Series

Dante's Inferno: *A Discussion Guide*
Dante's Paradise: *A Discussion Guide*
Dante's Purgatory: *A Discussion Guide*
Forrest Carter's The Education of Little Tree: *A Discussion Guide*
Homer's Iliad: *A Discussion Guide*
Homer's Odyssey: *A Discussion Guide*
Jane Austen's Pride and Prejudice: *A Discussion Guide*
Jerry Spinelli's Maniac Magee: *A Discussion Guide*
Jerry Spinelli's Stargirl: *A Discussion Guide*
Jonathan Swift's "A Modest Proposal": *A Discussion Guide*

Lloyd Alexander's The Black Cauldron: *A Discussion Guide*

Lloyd Alexander's The Book of Three: *A Discussion Guide*

Lois Lowry's Number the Stars: *A Discussion Guide*

Mark Twain's Adventures of Huckleberry Finn: *A Discussion Guide*

Mark Twain's The Adventures of Tom Sawyer: *A Discussion Guide*

Mark Twain's A Connecticut Yankee in King Arthur's Court: *A Discussion Guide*

Mark Twain's The Prince and the Pauper: *A Discussion Guide*

Nancy Garden's Annie on My Mind: *A Discussion Guide*

Nicholas Sparks' A Walk to Remember: *A Discussion Guide*

Virgil's Aeneid: *A Discussion Guide*

Virgil's "The Fall of Troy": A Discussion Guide

Voltaire's Candide: *A Discussion Guide*

William Shakespeare's 1 Henry IV: *A Discussion Guide*

William Shakespeare's Macbeth: *A Discussion Guide*

William Shakespeare's A Midsummer Night's Dream: *A Discussion Guide*

William Shakespeare's Romeo and Juliet: *A Discussion Guide*

William Sleator's Oddballs: *A Discussion Guide*

(Oddballs is an excellent source for teaching how to write autobiographical essays/personal narratives.)

Retellings of a Classic Work of Literature

Arden of Faversham: *A Retelling*

Ben Jonson's The Alchemist: *A Retelling*

Ben Jonson's The Arraignment, or Poetaster: *A Retelling*

Ben Jonson's Bartholomew Fair: *A Retelling*

Ben Jonson's The Case is Altered: *A Retelling*

Ben Jonson's Catiline's Conspiracy: *A Retelling*

Ben Jonson's The Devil is an Ass: *A Retelling*

Ben Jonson's Epicene: *A Retelling*

Ben Jonson's Every Man in His Humor: *A Retelling*

Ben Jonson's Every Man Out of His Humor: *A Retelling*

Ben Jonson's The Fountain of Self-Love, or Cynthia's Revels: *A Retelling*

Ben Jonson's The Magnetic Lady, or Humors Reconciled: *A Retelling*

Ben Jonson's The New Inn, or The Light Heart: *A Retelling*

Ben Jonson's Sejanus' Fall: *A Retelling*

Ben Jonson's The Staple of News: *A Retelling*

Ben Jonson's A Tale of a Tub: *A Retelling*

Ben Jonson's Volpone, or the Fox: *A Retelling*

Christopher Marlowe's Complete Plays: Retellings

Christopher Marlowe's Dido, Queen of Carthage: *A Retelling*

Christopher Marlowe's Doctor Faustus: *Retellings of the 1604 A-Text and of the 1616 B-Text*

Christopher Marlowe's Edward II: *A Retelling*

Christopher Marlowe's The Massacre at Paris: *A Retelling*

Christopher Marlowe's The Rich Jew of Malta: *A Retelling*

Christopher Marlowe's Tamburlaine, Parts 1 and 2: *Retellings*

Dante's Divine Comedy: *A Retelling in Prose*

Dante's Inferno: *A Retelling in Prose*

Dante's Purgatory: *A Retelling in Prose*

Dante's Paradise: *A Retelling in Prose*

The Famous Victories of Henry V: *A Retelling*

From the Iliad *to the* Odyssey: *A Retelling in Prose of Quintus of Smyrna's* Posthomerica

George Chapman, Ben Jonson, and John Marston's Eastward Ho! *A Retelling*

George Peele's The Arraignment of Paris: *A Retelling*

George Peele's The Battle of Alcazar: *A Retelling*

George Peele's David and Bathsheba, and the Tragedy of Absalom: *A Retelling*

George Peele's Edward I: *A Retelling*

George Peele's The Old Wives' Tale: *A Retelling*

George-a-Greene: *A Retelling*

The History of King Leir: *A Retelling*

Homer's Iliad: *A Retelling in Prose*

Homer's Odyssey: *A Retelling in Prose*

J.W. Gent.'s The Valiant Scot: *A Retelling*

Jason and the Argonauts: A Retelling in Prose of Apollonius of Rhodes' Argonautica

John Ford: Eight Plays Translated into Modern English

John Ford's The Broken Heart: *A Retelling*

John Ford's The Fancies, Chaste and Noble: *A Retelling*

John Ford's The Lady's Trial: *A Retelling*

John Ford's The Lover's Melancholy: *A Retelling*

John Ford's Love's Sacrifice: *A Retelling*

John Ford's Perkin Warbeck: *A Retelling*

John Ford's The Queen: *A Retelling*

John Ford's 'Tis Pity She's a Whore: *A Retelling*

John Lyly's Campaspe: *A Retelling*

John Lyly's Endymion, The Man in the Moon: *A Retelling*

John Lyly's Galatea: *A Retelling*

John Lyly's Love's Metamorphosis: *A Retelling*

John Lyly's Midas: *A Retelling*

John Lyly's Mother Bombie: *A Retelling*

John Lyly's Sappho and Phao: *A Retelling*

John Lyly's The Woman in the Moon: *A Retelling*

John Webster's The White Devil: *A Retelling*

King Edward III: *A Retelling*

Mankind: *A Medieval Morality Play* (A Retelling)

Margaret Cavendish's The Unnatural Tragedy: *A Retelling*

The Merry Devil of Edmonton: *A Retelling*

The Summoning of Everyman: *A Medieval Morality Play* (A Retelling)

Robert Greene's Friar Bacon and Friar Bungay: *A Retelling*

The Taming of a Shrew: *A Retelling*

Tarlton's Jests: A Retelling

Thomas Middleton's A Chaste Maid in Cheapside: *A Retelling*

Thomas Middleton's Women Beware Women: *A Retelling*

Thomas Middleton and Thomas Dekker's The Roaring Girl: *A Retelling*

Thomas Middleton and William Rowley's The Changeling: *A Retelling*

The Trojan War and Its Aftermath: Four Ancient Epic Poems

Virgil's Aeneid: *A Retelling in Prose*

William Shakespeare's 5 Late Romances: Retellings in Prose

William Shakespeare's 10 Histories: Retellings in Prose

William Shakespeare's 11 Tragedies: Retellings in Prose

William Shakespeare's 12 Comedies: Retellings in Prose

William Shakespeare's 38 Plays: Retellings in Prose

William Shakespeare's 1 Henry IV, aka Henry IV, Part 1: *A Retelling in Prose*

William Shakespeare's 2 Henry IV, aka Henry IV, Part 2: *A Retelling in Prose*

William Shakespeare's 1 Henry VI, aka Henry VI, Part 1: *A Retelling in Prose*

William Shakespeare's 2 Henry VI, aka Henry VI, Part 2: *A Retelling in Prose*

William Shakespeare's 3 Henry VI, aka Henry VI, Part 3: *A Retelling in Prose*

William Shakespeare's All's Well that Ends Well: *A Retelling in Prose*

William Shakespeare's Antony and Cleopatra: *A Retelling in Prose*

William Shakespeare's As You Like It: *A Retelling in Prose*

William Shakespeare's The Comedy of Errors: *A Retelling in Prose*

William Shakespeare's Coriolanus: *A Retelling in Prose*

William Shakespeare's Cymbeline: *A Retelling in Prose*

William Shakespeare's Hamlet: *A Retelling in Prose*

William Shakespeare's Henry V: *A Retelling in Prose*

William Shakespeare's Henry VIII: *A Retelling in Prose*

William Shakespeare's Julius Caesar: *A Retelling in Prose*

William Shakespeare's King John: *A Retelling in Prose*

William Shakespeare's King Lear: *A Retelling in Prose*

William Shakespeare's Love's Labor's Lost: *A Retelling in Prose*

William Shakespeare's Macbeth: *A Retelling in Prose*

William Shakespeare's Measure for Measure: *A Retelling in Prose*

William Shakespeare's The Merchant of Venice: *A Retelling in Prose*

William Shakespeare's The Merry Wives of Windsor: *A Retelling in Prose*

William Shakespeare's A Midsummer Night's Dream: *A Retelling in Prose*

William Shakespeare's Much Ado About Nothing: *A Retelling in Prose*

William Shakespeare's Othello: *A Retelling in Prose*

William Shakespeare's Pericles, Prince of Tyre: *A Retelling in Prose*

William Shakespeare's Richard II: *A Retelling in Prose*

William Shakespeare's Richard III: *A Retelling in Prose*

William Shakespeare's Romeo and Juliet: *A Retelling in Prose*

William Shakespeare's The Taming of the Shrew: *A Retelling in Prose*

William Shakespeare's The Tempest: *A Retelling in Prose*

William Shakespeare's Timon of Athens: *A Retelling in Prose*

William Shakespeare's Titus Andronicus: *A Retelling in Prose*

William Shakespeare's Troilus and Cressida: *A Retelling in Prose*

William Shakespeare's Twelfth Night: *A Retelling in Prose*

William Shakespeare's The Two Gentlemen of Verona: *A Retelling in Prose*

William Shakespeare's The Two Noble Kinsmen: *A Retelling in Prose*

APPENDIX D: SOME BOOKS BY BRENDA KENNEDY (MY SISTER)

The Forgotten Trilogy
    Book One: *Forgetting the Past*
    Book Two: *Living for Today*
    Book Three: *Seeking the Future*
The Learning to Live Trilogy
    Book One: *Learning to Live*
    Book Two: *Learning to Trust*
    Book Three: *Learning to Love*
The Starting Over Trilogy
    Book One: *A New Beginning*
    Book Two: *Saving Angel*
    Book Three: *Destined to Love*
The Freedom Trilogy
    Book One: *Shattered Dreams*
    Book Two: *Broken Lives*
    Book Three: *Mending Hearts*
The Fighting to Survive Trilogy
    Round One: *A Life Worth Fighting*
    Round Two: *Against the Odds*
    Round Three: *One Last Fight*
The Rose Farm Trilogy
    Book One: *Forever Country*
    Book Two: *Country Life*
    Book Three: *Country Love*
Books in the Seashell Island Stand-alone Series
    Book One: *Home on Seashell Island* (Free)
    Book Two: *Christmas on Seashell Island*
    Book Three: *Living on Seashell Island*
    Book Four: *Moving to Seashell Island*
    Book Five: *Returning to Seashell Island*
Books in the Pineapple Grove Cozy Murder Mystery Stand-alone Series
    Book One: *Murder Behind the Coffeehouse*
Books in the Montgomery Wine Stand-alone Series
    Book One: *A Place to Call Home*

Book Two: *In Search of Happiness...* coming soon

Stand-alone books in the "Another Round of Laughter Series" written by Brenda and some of her siblings: Carla Evans, Martha Farmer, Rosa Jones, and David Bruce.

Cupcakes Are Not a Diet Food (Free)

Kids Are Not Always Angels

Aging Is Not for Sissies

[1] Source: Michael Moore, *Here Comes Trouble: Stories from my Life*, pp. 5-9, 31-32.

[2] Source: Richard Roeper, "Friendly advice for the prez: Just quit ... Smoking, that is—after all, he ranks as true role model." *Chicago Sun-Times*. 2 March 2010 <http://www.suntimes.com/news/roeper/2077815,CST-NWS-roep02.article>.

[3] Source: Froma Harrop, "Score One for Consumers." Creators Syndicate. 10 April 2007 <http://www.creators.com/opinion/froma-harrop/score-one-for-consumers.htmlScore One for Consumers>.

[4] Source: Karen Olsson, "Noomi Rapace Arrives in Hollywood, by Way of Outer Space." *New York Times Magazine*. 27 May 2012 <http://www.nytimes.com/2012/05/27/magazine/noomi-rapace-arrives-in-hollywood-by-way-of-outer-space.html?_r=1&pagewanted=1>.

[5] Source: Luaine Lee, "Jamie Kaler and his 'Boys' return Thursday to TBS." McClatchy-Tribune News Service. 9 June 2008 <http://www.popmatters.com/pm/news/article/59563/jamie-kaler-and-his-boys-return-thursday-to-tbs/>.

[6] Source: Interview by Jack Watkins, "Tom Baker: how I made *Doctor Who*." *Guardian*. 4 November 2013 <http://www.theguardian.com/tv-and-radio/2013/nov/04/how-i-made-doctor-who>.

[7] Source: Virginia Aronson, *Jennifer Love Hewitt*, pp. 13, 31, 35-36.

[8] Source: Stephen Tobolowsky, "Memories of the 'Sneakers' Shoot." *Slate*. 10 September 2012 <http://www.slate.com/articles/arts/culturebox/2012/09/robert_redford_sidney_poitier_ben_kingsley_dan_aykroyd_what_it_was_like_shooting

[9] Source: Stephen Moss, "Michael Winner: 'The only purpose of life is to avoid boredom.'" *The Guardian*. 16 November 2009 <http://www.guardian.co.uk/film/2009/nov/16/michael-winner-restaurants-death-boredom>.

[10] Source: Rebecca Stefoff, *Mary Tyler Moore: The Woman Behind the Smile*, p. 36.

[11] Source: David Hiltbrand, "She's Sarah, one tough mother — but will she be terminated?" *The Philadelphia Inquirer*. 22 February 2008 <http://www.popmatters.com/pm/news/article/55354/shes-sarah-one-tough-mother-but-will-she-be-terminated/>.

[12] Source: Mel Blanc and Philip Bashe, *That's Not All, Folks*, pp. 66-67.

[13] Source: John Anderson, "Supporting actress nomination raises Amy Ryan's profile." *Newsday*. 28 January 2008 <http://www.popmatters.com/pm/news/article/53613/supporting-actress-nomination-raises-amy-ryans-profile/>.

[14] Source: Paul Parla and Charles P. Mitchell, *Screen Sirens Scream!*, pp. 225, 236.

[15] Source: Randi Reisfeld and Marie Morreale, *Got Issues Much: Celebrities Share Their Traumas and Triumphs*, pp. 43-45.

[16] Source: Will Harris, "A Chat with Saul Rubinek, Co-star of *Warehouse 13*." 7 July 2009 <http://www.bullz-eye.com/television/interviews/2009/saul_rubinek.htm>.

[17] Source: Alan Jackson, "Blanchett juggles blockbusters and babies." Times Online. May 2010 <http://entertainment.timesonline.co.uk/tol/arts_and_entertainment/film/article7115564.ece>.

[18] Source: Don Knotts, *Barney Fife and Other Characters I Have Known*, p. 132.

[19] Source: Laura Barnett, "'Next!': the secretive world of casting directors." *Guardian* (UK). 21 May 2013 <http://www.guardian.co.uk/stage/2013/may/21/casting-directors>.

[20] Source: Peter Bradshaw, "Pete Postlethwaite: A face we won't forget." *The Guardian*. 4 January 2011 <http://www.guardian.co.uk/film/2011/jan/04/pete-postlethwaite-film-actor>.

[21] Source: Dave Rogers, *The Avengers*, p. 133.

[22] Source: Joe Franklin, *Up Late with Joe Franklin*, p. 228.

[23] Source: Alex Godfrey, "Sissy Spacek: 'I was fearless.'" *Guardian*. 19 March 2015 <http://tinyurl.com/ng5hm5u>.

[24] Source: Richard Schickel, *Cary Grant: A Celebration*, p. 41.

[25] Source: Alex Godfrey, "Sissy Spacek: 'I was fearless.'" *Guardian*. 19 March 2015 <http://tinyurl.com/ng5hm5u>.

[26] Source: Kevin Spacey, "Foreward" to Chris Lemmon's *A Twist of Lemmon: A Tribute to My Father*, p. x, Also, Chris Lemmon, *A Twist of Lemmon: A Tribute to My Father*, p. 193.

[27] Source: Dick Cavett, *Talk Show: Confrontations, Pointed Commentary, and Off-Screen Secrets*, p. 36.

[28] Source: Boze Hadleigh, *Hollywood Gays*, p. 287.

[29] Source: Edward Edelsen, *Tough Guys and Gals of the Movies*, p. 102.

[30] Source: Patrick Goldstein, "Roger Corman: Hollywood's original low-budget superhero." *Los Angeles Times*. 13 December 2011 <http://latimesblogs.latimes.com/movies/2011/12/roger-corman-indy-hollywoods-original-superhero.html>.

[31] Source: Jim and Henny Backus, *Forgive Us Our Digressions*, pp. 83-85.

[32] Source: Glenhall Taylor, *Before Television*, pp. 31-32.

[33] Source: Bernice Kanner, *The 100 Best TV Commercials*, p. 214.

[34] Source: Amy Boothe Green and Howard E. Green, *Remembering Walt: Favorite Memories of Walt Disney*, pp. 37, 81, 159.

[35] Source: Chuck Jones, *Chuck Redux: Drawing from the Fun Side of Life*, pp. 181-182.

[36] Source: Will Harris, "A Chat with Philip Baker Hall." Bullz-eye.com. 8 August 2008 <http://www.bullz-eye.com/movies/interviews/2008/philip_baker_hall.htm>.

[37] Source: Joe Franklin, *Up Late with Joe Franklin*, p. 182.

[38] Source: "The 25 Most Powerful TV Shows of the Last 25 Years." *Mental Floss*. 12 October 2012 <http://www.mentalfloss.com/blogs/archives/146530#ixzz29Gxwx3gR>.

[39] Source: Kevin J. Hayes, editor, *Charlie Chaplin: Interviews*, p. 29.

[40] Source: Lionel Rolfe, "Tales of an Extraordinary Madman." *Random Lengths*. 21 May 2010 <http://www.randomlengthsnews.com/content/view/458/83/>.

[41] Source: Larry Kettelkamp, *Bill Cosby: Family Funny Man*, pp. 81, 83.

[42] Source: Gerald Nachman, *Seriously Funny*, p. 347.

[43] Source: Joe Garner, *Made You Laugh*, p. 53.

[44] Source: Brooks Barnes, "The Thing That Ate Saturday Night." *New York Times*. 14 January 2011 <http://www.nytimes.com/2011/01/16/arts/television/16syfy.html?ref=arts>.

[45] Source: Joe Garagiola, *It's Anybody's Ballgame*, p. 229.

[46] Source: HENRY ROLLINS, "I JUST SPENT A WEEK COVERED IN BLOOD." *Los Angeles Weekly*. 25 June 2015 <http://tinyurl.com/pbphasa>.

[47] Source: Sara McIntosh Wooten, *Oprah Winfrey: Talk Show Legend*, p. 42.

[48] Source: Anita Sethi, "Prunella Scales: My family values." *Guardian*. 14 June 2013 <http://www.guardian.co.uk/lifeandstyle/2013/jun/14/prunella-scales-timothy-west-family-values>.

[49] Source: Chuck Jones, *Chuck Amok: The Life and Times of an Animated Cartoonist*, pp. 215, 285.

[50] Source: Frank McGuinness, "When Greta Garbo came to town." *The Guardian*. 11 January 2010 <http://www.guardian.co.uk/stage/2010/jan/11/greta-garbo-donegal-frank-mcguinness>.

[51] Source: Allan Neuwirth, *They'll Never Put That on the Air*, p. 166.

[52] Source: Bill Hanna, *A Cast of Friends*, pp. 7-8, 15

[53] Source: Mike Bonner, *Jennifer Aniston*, pp. 16-18, 28, 50.

[54] Source: Chuck Norris, *The Official Chuck Norris Fact Book*, pp. 39, 50, 165.

[55] Source: Raymond H. Miller, *Matt Groening*, pp. 8-9.

[56] Source: Ed McMahon, *For Laughing Out Loud: My Life and Good Times*, pp. 88-89.

[57] Source: Myrna Oliver and Valerie J. Nelson, "Art Linkletter dies at 97; broadcasting pioneer created 'Kids Say the Darndest Things.'" *Los Angeles Times.* 27 May 2010 <http://www.latimes.com/news/obituaries/la-me-art-linkletter-new-20100527,0,4838362,full.story>.

[58] Source: Mary Malone, *Connie Chung: Broadcast Journalist*, pp. 9, 11, 13.

[59] Source: Katie Couric, *The Best Advice I Ever Got: Lessons from Extraordinary Lives*, pp. xvii, xxiv.

[60] Source: Chuck Jones, *Chuck Amok: The Life and Times of an Animated Cartoonist*, pp. 234-235.

[61] Source: Ed McMahon, *Here's Johnny! My Memories of Johnny Carson, The Tonight Show, and 46 Years of Friendship*, pp. 175-177.

[62] Source: Barbara Feldon, *Living Alone and Loving It*, pp. 53-54.

[63] Source: Roger Ebert, "Virginia, Michael & Elaine Madsen: From Chicago to their dreams." *Chicago Sun-Times.* From June 13, 1986; revised 11/17/08. <http://rogerebert.suntimes.com/apps/pbcs.dll/article?AID=/19860613/PEOPLE/811189998/1023>.

[64] Source: Groucho Marx, *The Secret Word is Groucho*, p. 83.

[65] Source: Willa Paskin, "The Muppets Reboot Ruined Miss Piggy." Slate. 21 September 2015 <http://tinyurl.com/or4gfvk>.

[66] Source: Luaine Lee, "Travis Fimmel milks his role on 'The Beast' for all it's worth." McClatchy-Tribune News Service. 26 January 2009 <http://www.popmatters.com/pm/article/69595-travis-fimmel-milks-his-role-on-the-beast-for-all-its-worth/>.

[67] Source: Norma Jean Lutz, *Britney Spears*, p. 27.

[68] Source: Kermit Schafer, *The Bedside Book of Celebrity Bloopers*, p. 10.

[69] Source: Arthur Marx, *Red Skelton*, pp. 182, 186-187, 263-264.

[70] Source: Ben Primack, adapter and editor, *The Ben Hecht Show*, p. 127.

[71] Source: David Brown, *Star Billing: Tell-Tale Trivia from Hollywood*, pp. 82-83.

[72] Source: Anita Loos, *Kiss Hollywood Goodbye*, pp. 138, 141-142.

[73] Source: Stephen Schochet, *Hollywood Stories*, pp. 189-190.

[74] Source: Ron Smith, *Comic Support*, p. 7.

[75] Source: Ginny Weissman and Coyne Steven Sanders, *The Dick Van Dyke Show*, pp. 40. 43.

[76] Source: Rebecca Stefoff, *Mary Tyler Moore: The Woman Behind the Smile*, p. 30.

[77] Source: Patty Fox, *Star Style: Hollywood Legends as Fashion Icons*, p. 59.

[78] Source: Robert Pegg, *Comical Co-Stars of Television*, p. 55.

[79] Source: Ed McMahon, *Here's Johnny! My Memories of Johnny Carson, The Tonight Show, and 46 Years of Friendship*, pp. 34, 112-113, 129.

[80] Source: Yael Kohen, *We Killed: The Rise of Women in American Comedy*, pp. 108, 115.

[81] Source: Marlo Thomas, *Growing Up Laughing: My Story and the Story of Funny*, p. 291.

[82] Source: Michael Munn, "The rage behind McQueen." *Sunday Times*. 18 April 2010 <http://entertainment.timesonline.co.uk/tol/arts_and_entertainment/books/book_extracts/article7100746.ece>. An edited extract from *Steve McQueen: Living on the Edge*, by Michael Munn.

[83] Source: Jim Harmon, *The Great Radio Heroes*, p. 51.

[84] Source: Martyn Palmer, "Kiefer Sutherland: prison changed me." *The Times*. 27 September 2008 <http://entertainment.timesonline.co.uk/tol/arts_and_entertainment/film/article4802328.ece>.

[85] Source: Amy Hollingsworth, *The Simple Faith of Mister Rogers*, p. 129.

[86] Source: Roger Ebert, "Answer Man: Long & short of 'Bourne.'" 9 August 2007 <http://rogerebert.suntimes.com/apps/pbcs.dll/section?category=ANSWERMAN>.

[87] Source: Lawrence Grobel, *Above the Line: Conversations About the Movies*, p. 347.

[88] Source: Lawrence J. Epstein, *George Burns: An American Life*, p.184.

[89] Source: Amy Chozick, "Quiet on the Small Set." *Wall Street Journal*. 6 May 2011 <http://online.wsj.com/article/SB10001424052748703849204576303230454566852.html?mod=WSJ_ArtsEnt_Lifes

[90] Source: Colin Covert, "'Gilliam Curse' continues with 'Imaginarium of Doctor Parnassus.'" *Star Tribune* (Minneapolis, MN). 8 January 2010 <http://www.popmatters.com/pm/article/118658-gilliam-curse-continues-with-imaginarium-of-doctor-parnassus/>.

[91] Source: Joe Bob Briggs, *Profoundly Disturbing: Shocking Movies That Changed History!*, pp. 220, 225-226.

[92] Source: Paula Marantz Cohen, "Alfred Hitchcock: modest exhibitionist." *The Times*. 5 September 2008 <http://entertainment.timesonline.co.uk/tol/arts_and_entertainment/the_tls/article4685615.ece>.

[93] Source: Peter Bogdanovich, *Peter Bogdanovich's Movie of the Week*, p. 40.

[94] Source: Roger Ebert, "Awake in the Dark: Best of Ebert." 19 September 2006 <http://rogerebert.suntimes.com/apps/pbcs.dll/article?AID=/20060919/COMMENTARY/60919001>.

[95] Source: Peter Bogdanovich, *Peter Bogdanovich's Movie of the Week*, pp. 57-58.

[96] Source: Kristen A. Graham, "Tony Danza says his class act isn't just for show." *The Philadelphia Inquirer*. 10 March 2010 <http://www.popmatters.com/pm/article/122117-tony-danza-says-his-class-act-isnt-just-for-show/>.

[97] Source: John Patterson: "Airplane at 30! The ride of their lives." *The Guardian*. 22 August 2010 <http://www.guardian.co.uk/film/2010/aug/22/airplane-at-30-zucker-abrahams-interview>.

[98] Source: Katie Couric, *The Best Advice I Ever Got: Lessons from Extraordinary Lives*, pp. 170-171.

[99] Source: Darryl Lyman, *The Jewish Comedy Catalog*, p. 177.

[100] Source: Marlo Thomas, *Growing Up Laughing: My Story and the Story of Funny*, pp. 488-490.

[101] Source: Robert Pegg, *Comical Co-Stars of Television*, p. 64.

[102] Source: David Medsher, "A Chat with Christopher McDonald, Co-star of *Splinterheads* and *Happy Gilmore*." Bullz-Eye.com. 25 February 2010 <http://www.bullz-eye.com/movies/interviews/2010/christopher_mcdonald.htm>.

[103] Source: Luaine Lee, "Thanks to one special fan, Uhura became a lifetime role for Nichelle Nichols." McClatchy-Tribune News Service. 5 January 2011 <http://www.popmatters.com/pm/article/135446-thanks-to-one-special-fan-uhura-became-a-lifetime-role-for-nichelle-/>.

[104] Source: Charles Grodin, et al. *If I Only Knew Then ... Learning from Our Mistakes*, pp. 7-10.

[105] Source: Jamie Farr, *Just Farr Fun*, pp. 12, 236.

[106] Source: Lydia Martin, "Rita Moreno overcame Hispanic stereotypes to achieve stardom." McClatchy Newspapers. 18 September 2008 < http://www.popmatters.com/pm/article/63543/rita-moreno-overcame-hispanic-stereotypes-to-achieve-stardom/ >.

[107] Source: Virginia Aronson, *Jennifer Love Hewitt*, pp. 56-57.

[108] Source: Amy Boothe Green and Howard E. Green, *Remembering Walt: Favorite Memories of Walt Disney*, pp. 162-163.

[109] Source: Kerry Diamond, *Kevyn Aucoin: A Beautiful Life*, p. 128.

[110] Source: Lawrence Grobel, *Above the Line: Conversations About the Movies*, p. 343.

[111] Source: Cynthia Laslo *Sarah Michelle Gellar*

[112] Source: "Beauty & the Beast." YouTube. <http://www.youtube.com/watch?v=oeoPtz0F2Ck>. Accessed 21 November 2010.

[113] Source: Bill Adler and Bruce Cassiday, *The World of Jay Leno: His Humor and His Life*, p. 206.

[114] Source: Joe Garner, *Made You Laugh*, p. 20.

[115] Source: Gerald Nachman, *Seriously Funny*, p. 120.

[116] Source: Terri Dougherty, *Ashton Kutcher*, pp. 19, 89.

[117] Source: Larry Kettelkamp, *Bill Cosby: Family Funny Man*, p. 59.

[118] Source: Kermit Schafer, *The Bedside Book of Celebrity Bloopers*, pp. 74-75.

[119] Source: Roseanne Barr, "Fame's a bitch. It's hard to handle and drives you nuts." *Guardian*. 11 June 2011 <http://www.guardian.co.uk/culture/2011/jun/11/roseanne-barr-on-fame>.

[120] Source: Will Harris, "Andrew Zimmern, Host of *Bizarre Foods*." Bullz-eye.com. 31 August 2009 <http://www.bullz-eye.com/television/interviews/2009/andrew_zimmern.htm>.

[121] Source: Zachary Pincus-Roth, "YouTube creative artists pride themselves on being a separate breed." *Los Angeles Times*. Accessed 19 September 2010 <http://www.latimes.com/entertainment/news/la-ca-video-stars19-20100919,0,5743139,full.story>.

[122] Source: John Lichfield, "France mourns Claude Chabrol, giant of cinema's New Wave." *The Independent*. 13 September 2010 <chabrol-giant-of-cinemas-new-wave-2077552.html>.

[123] Source: Paul Mason, *Sarah Michelle Gellar*, p. 8.

[124] Source: Herb Sanford, *Ladies and Gentlemen, The Garry Moore Show: Behind the Scenes When TV was New*, p. 78.

[125] Source: Mel Blanc and Philip Bashe, *That's Not All, Folks*, pp. 1-3, 84, 237-238.

[126] Source: Kerry Diamond, *Kevyn Aucoin: A Beautiful Life*, pp. 175, 194.

[127] Source: Howard Bragman, "Paper Trail: How to Come Out." *The Advocate*. 20 January 2009 <http://www.advocate.com/exclusive_detail_ektid70585.asp>.

[128] Source: Michael Fairman, "How to Tell Your Parents You're Gay." *The Advocate*. 9 September 2009 <http://www.advocate.com/Arts_and_Entertainment/Television/How_to_Tell_Your_Parents_You__39;re_Gay/>.

[129] Source: Brent Hartinger, "Neil Patrick Harris Lets it all Hang Out." Afterelton.com. 17 June 2008 <http://www.afterelton.com/people/2008/6/neilpatrickharris>.

[130] Source: Michael Jensen, "Interview with George Takei and Brad Altman. Afterelton.com. 18 June 2008 <http://www.afterelton.com/people/2008/6/georgetakei_bradaltman>.

[131] Source: James Hillis, "Interview with *Will & Grace*'s Max Mutchnick." 5 March 2008 <http://www.afterelton.com/people/2008/3/maxmutchnick>.

[132] Source: Camilla Redmond, "Writing the Century." *The Guardian*. 20 April 2010 <http://www.guardian.co.uk/tv-and-radio/2010/apr/20/writing-the-century-review>.

[133] Source: "Memories of Coming Out." *The Advocate*. 7 October 2008 <http://www.advocate.com/exclusive_detail_ektid63152.asp>.

[134] Source: Dominic Wells, "Dale Winton: No one ever asked if I was gay." *The Times*. 17 September 2008 <http://entertainment.timesonline.co.uk/tol/arts_and_entertainment/tv_and_radio/article4767255.ece>.

[135] Source: Graham Kolbeins, "Gay TV Scribes Prove Life Really Is Golden." *The Advocate*. 7 November 2008 <http://www.advocate.com/exclusive_detail_ektid65277.asp>.

[136] Source: Ed McMahon, *For Laughing Out Loud: My Life and Good Times*, pp. 285-286.

[137] Source: Margaret L. Finn, *Mary Tyler Moore*, pp. 26, 113.

[138] Source: David Brown, *Star Billing: Tell-Tale Trivia from Hollywood*, p. 101.

[139] Source: Terri Dougherty, *Ashton Kutcher*, pp. 21, 65.

[140] Source: Jim and Henny Backus, *Forgive Us Our Digressions*, pp. 18-19.

[141] Source: Michael Moore, *Here Comes Trouble: Stories from my Life*, pp. 380-384.

[142] Source: Mike Walker, "HATHAWAY CLUELESS ABOUT HOMELESS." *National Enquirer*. 6 October 2009 <http://www.nationalenquirer.com/mike-walker/hathaway-clueless-about-homeless>. Also: Mike Walker, "SOBERING SCENE: KIEFER RESCUES DRUNK," *National Enquirer*. 23 November 2010 <http://www.nationalenquirer.com/mike-walker/sobering-scene-kiefer-rescues-drunk>. Also: Mike Walker, "JESSICA ALBA SAVES THE DAY," *National Enquirer*. 14 September 2005 <http://www.nationalenquirer.com/mike-walker/jessica-alba-saves-day-0>.

[143] Source: Richard Zoglin, *Comedy at the Edge: How Stand-up in the 1970s Changed America*, p. 143.

[144] Source: Lila and Rick Guzmán, *George Lopez: Latino King*, pp. 52, 75-77.

[145] Source: Soupy Sales, *Soupy Sez! My Zany Life and Times*, pp. 201-202.

[146] Source: "The 25 Most Powerful TV Shows of the Last 25 Years." *Mental Floss*. 12 October 2012 <http://www.mentalfloss.com/blogs/archives/146530#ixzz29Gxwx3gR>.

[147] Source: "RENEE ZELLWEGER OPENS HER HEART TO HOMELESS MAN." *National Enquirer*. 18 December 2001

<http://www.nationalenquirer.com/celebrity/renee-zellweger-opens-her-heart-homeless-man>.

[148] Source: Richard Zoglin, *Comedy at the Edge: How Stand-up in the 1970s Changed America*, p. 94.

[149] Source: Fred Rogers, *You Are Special*, p. 104.

[150] Source: Bill Adler, *Jewish Wit and Wisdom*, p. 61.

[151] Source: Maureen Furniss, editor, *Chuck Jones Conversations*, p. 9.

[152] Source: Ron Smith, *Comic Support*, p. 226.

[153] Source: Gene Adair, *Alfred Hitchcock: Filming Our Fears*, pp. 24, 29, 51, 53, 79-80, 97.

[154] Source: Elaine Lipworth, "Jeff Bridges: My family values." *The Guardian*. 19 June 2010 <http://www.guardian.co.uk/lifeandstyle/2010/jun/19/jeff-bridges-my-family-values>.

[155] Source: Lila and Rick Guzmán, *George Lopez: Latino King*, p, pp. 32-33, 35.

[156] Source: Anita Loos, *Kiss Hollywood Goodbye*, pp. 51-52.

[157] Source: Gina Piccalo, "For Betty White, a career on the sly." *Los Angeles Times*. 6 January 2010 <http://theenvelope.latimes.com/news/more/print/la-en-betty-white6-2010jan06,0,424445.story>.

[158] Source: Maureen Furniss, editor, *Chuck Jones Conversations*, pp. 34-35.

[159] Source: Aaron Barnhart, "MSNBC's Keith Olbermann enjoys big success and a little wisdom." McClatchy Newspapers. 8 January 2008 <http://www.popmatters.com/pm/news/article/52879/msnbcs-keith-olbermann-enjoys-big-success-and-a-little-wisdom/>.

[160] Source: Sam McManis, "NPR's Schorr a vital link to 'responsible journalism.'" McClatchy Newspapers. 17 January 2008 <http://www.popmatters.com/pm/news/article/53157/nprs-schorr-a-vital-link-to-responsible-journalism/>.

[161] Source: Yael Kohen, *We Killed: The Rise of Women in American Comedy*, p. 79.

[162] Source: Joe Bob Briggs, *Profoundly Disturbing: Shocking Movies That Changed History!*, p. 160.

[163] Source: Vince Waldron, *Classic Sitcoms*, p. 344.

[164] Source: Kermit Schafer, *All Time Great Bloopers*, p. 96.

[165] Source: Barbara Feldon, *Living Alone and Loving It*, p. 128.

[166] Source: Richard Kelly, *The Andy Griffith Show*, p. 109.

[167] Source: Chris Lemmon, *A Twist of Lemmon: A Tribute to My Father*, pp. 42-43/

[168] Source: Mary Malone, *Connie Chung: Broadcast Journalist*, pp. 28, 54.

[169] Source: May Wale Brown, *Reel Life on Hollywood Movie Sets*, pp. 103-104.

[170] Source: Susan King, "Classic Hollywood: Piper Laurie." *Los Angeles Times*. 29 September 2010 <http://www.latimes.com/entertainment/news/la-et-classic-hollywood-20100929,0,7754114.story>.

[171] Source: Joseph V. Amodio, "Fast chat with 'The Happening' co-star John Leguizamo. *Newsday*. 12 June 2008 <http://www.popmatters.com/pm/news/article/59692/fast-chat-with-the-happening-co-star-john-leguizamo/>.

[172] Source: Jimmy Crum and Carole Gerber, *How About That!*, p. 6.

[173] Source: Bernice Kanner, *The 100 Best TV Commercials*, pp. 45-46.

[174] Source: Kermit Schafer, *All Time Great Bloopers*, p. 62.

[175] Source: Luaine Lee, "After near death, Jane Seymour is getting the most out of life." McClatchy-Tribune News Service. 19 August 2008 <http://www.popmatters.com/pm/article/62274/after-near-death-jane-seymour-is-getting-the-most-out-of-life/>.

[176] Source: Bill Hanna, *A Cast of Friends*, pp. 24-25.

[177] Source: Joseph Barbera, *My Life in 'toons: From Flatbush to Bedrock in Under a Century*, pp. 139-40.

[178] Source: Sarah Warn, "Making 'Ghostella's Haunted Tomb.'" AfterEllen. 14 May 2008 <http://www.afterellen.com/people/2008/5/ghostella>.

[179] Source: Tim Long, "What I did during the strike." *Los Angeles Times*. 13 February 2008 <http://www.latimes.com/news/opinion/commentary/la-oew-wgastrike13feb13,0,1083440.story>.

[180] Source: Jamie Farr, *Just Farr Fun*, pp. 274-275.

[181] Source: Martha Sigall, *Living Life Inside the Lines: Tales from the Golden Age of Animation*, p. 98.

[182] Source: Bill Adler and Bruce Cassiday, *The World of Jay Leno: His Humor and His Life*, p. 8.

[183] Source: Anne Saidman, *Oprah Winfrey: Media Success Story*, p. 12.

[184] Source: Ginny Weissman and Coyne Steven Sanders, *The Dick Van Dyke Show*, p. 22.

[185] Source: Kevin J. Hayes, editor, *Charlie Chaplin: Interviews*, p. 94.

[186] Source: Dave Rogers, *The Avengers*, p. 101.

[187] Source: John Patterson, "Danny Trejo, the Face that Launched a Thousand Bit Parts." *The Guardian*. 18 November 2010 <http://www.guardian.co.uk/film/2010/nov/18/danny-trejo-machete>.

[188] Source: Joseph Barbera, *My Life in 'toons: From Flatbush to Bedrock in Under a Century*, p. 133.

[189] Source: Brenda Scott Royce, *Hogan's Heroes*, pp. 60, 132.

[190] Source: Soupy Sales, *Soupy Sez! My Zany Life and Times*, pp. 14, 53.

[191] Source: Richard Schickel, *Cary Grant: A Celebration*, p. 39.

[192] Source: Craig McLean, "Why Miley Cyrus is the world's biggest-ever teenage star." *The Times*. 11 October 2008 <http://entertainment.timesonline.co.uk/tol/arts_and_entertainment/tv_and_radio/article4891217.ece >.

[193] Source: Joey Green, *The Get Smart Handbook*, p. 43.

[194] Source: Sara McIntosh Wooten, *Oprah Winfrey: Talk Show Legend*, pp. 13-14.

[195] Source: Elizabeth Day, "Kenneth Branagh: the king of comedy." *Guardian* (UK). 8 October 2011 <http://www.guardian.co.uk/culture/2011/oct/09/kenneth-branagh-the-painkiller-interview>.

[196] Source: Amy Hollingsworth, *The Simple Faith of Mister Rogers*, p. 19.

[197] Source: Andrew Tobias, "Money, PAC Money." 3 March 2009 <http://www.andrewtobias.com/newcolumns/090303.html>. Also: "Spitting Image." Consulted 4 February 2009 <http://en.wikiquote.org/wiki/Spitting_Image>.

[198] Source: Allan Neuwirth, *They'll Never Put That on the Air*, p. 75.

[199] Source: Karen Adir, *The Great Clowns of American Television*, pp. 109-110.

[200] Source: May Wale Brown, *Reel Life on Hollywood Movie Sets*, pp. 111-112.

[201] Source: Will Harris, "A Chat with Lisa Lackey, Co-star of *Heroes*." Bullz-eye.com. 14 July 2009 <http://www.bullz-eye.com/television/interviews/2009/lisa_lackey.htm>.

[202] Source: Glenhall Taylor, *Before Television*, p. 118.

[203] Source: Chuck Norris, *The Official Chuck Norris Fact Book*, pp. 233-235.

[204] Source: Richard Kelly, *The Andy Griffith Show*, pp. 35-36.

[205] Source: Ben Primack, adapter and editor, *The Ben Hecht Show*, p. 136.

[206] Source: Joe Garagiola, *It's Anybody's Ballgame*, p. 164.

[207] Source: Edith Head, and Paddy Calistro, *Edith Head's Hollywood*, pp. 24, 31, 140-141.

[208] Source: Sarah Feldberg, "Jerry Springer, American Dreamer." *Las Vegas Weekly*. 12 November 2009 <http://www.lasvegasweekly.com/news/2009/nov/12/jer-ry-jer-ry/>.

[209] Source: Lawrence J. Epstein, *George Burns: An American Life*, p. 136.

[210] Source: Margaret L. Finn, *Mary Tyler Moore*, pp. 84-85.

[211] Source: Raymond H. Miller, *Matt Groening*, p. 18.

[212] Source: Joel Stein, "My Emmy night on the red carpet: Catching stars for quick interviews on camera isn't as easy as it looks." *Los Angeles Times*. 21 September 2007 <http://www.latimes.com/news/opinion/commentary/la-oe-stein21sep21,0,7151837.column?coll=la-util-opinion-commentary>.

[213] Source: Bob Denver, *Gilligan, Maynard and Me*, p. 30.

[214] Source: Edith Head, and Paddy Calistro, *Edith Head's Hollywood*, pp. 71-72.

[215] Source: Patty Fox, *Star Style: Hollywood Legends as Fashion Icons*, p. 44.

[216] Source: Christopher Golden and Nancy Holder. *Buffy the Vampire Slayer: The Watcher's Guide*, p. 198.

[217] Source: Christopher Golden and Nancy Holder. *Buffy the Vampire Slayer: The Watcher's Guide*, p. 200.

[218] Source: Susan Edwards, *Erma Bombeck*, p. 17.

[219] Source: Xan Brooks. "Richard Linklater: 'I'm not like Orson Welles. I'm a quiet director.'" *The Guardian*. 1 December 2009 <http://www.guardian.co.uk/film/2009/dec/01/richard-linklater-orson-welles>.

[220] Source: Groucho Marx, *The Secret Word is Groucho*, pp. 135-136.

[221] Source: Darryl Lyman, *The Jewish Comedy Catalog*, p. 166.

[222] Source: "Lou Dates Mary," an episode of *The Mary Tyler Moore Show*.

[223] Source: Jim Emerson, "'Idiocracy' and the ten-best trolls." *Chicago Sun-Times* Blog (Illinois). 14 December 2011 <http://blogs.suntimes.com/scanners/2011/12/idiocracy_and_the_ten-best_.html>.

[224] Source: Nancy Rommelmann, "Review of *Backing Into Forward: A Memoir* by Jules Feiffer." Powells.com. Originally printed in *The Oregonian*. 8 April 2010 <http://www.powells.com/review/2010_04_08.html>.

[225] Source: Anita Gates, "Suzanne Pleshette, 70, 'Newhart' Actress, Dies." *The New York Times*. 21 January 2008 <http://www.nytimes.com/2008/01/21/arts/21cnd-pleshette.html?hp>. Also: Dennis McLellan, "Suzanne Pleshette, sultry-voiced comic partner of Newhart; dies at 70." *Los Angeles Times*. 21 January 2008 <http://www.boston.com/ae/celebrity/articles/2008/01/21/suzanne_pleshette_sultry_voiced_comic_partner_of_newhart_at_70/?page=1>.

[226] Source: Ginny Dougary, "Omid Djalili, seriously funny." *The Times*. 22 March 2008 <http://entertainment.timesonline.co.uk/tol/arts_and_entertainment/stage/comedy/article3590492.ece>.

[227] Source: Stephen Schochet, *Hollywood Stories*, p. 191.

[228] Source: Emma John: "This much I know: Tim Robbins," *The Guardian*. 26 September 2010 <http://www.guardian.co.uk/lifeandstyle/2010/sep/26/this-much-i-know-tim-robbins-rogues-gallery-band>.

[229] Source: Arthur Marx, *Red Skelton*, p. 66.

[230] Source: Luaine Lee, "Jamie Kaler and his 'Boys' return Thursday to TBS." McClatchy-Tribune News Service. 9 June 2008 <http://www.popmatters.com/pm/news/article/59563/jamie-kaler-and-his-boys-return-thursday-to-tbs/>.

[231] Source: Charles Grodin, et al. *If I Only Knew Then ... Learning from Our Mistakes*, pp. 25-26.

[232] Source: "Memories of Coming Out: Day 3." *The Advocate*. 9 October 2008 <http://www.advocate.com/exclusive_detail_ektid63298.asp>.

[233] Source: Randi Reisfeld and Marie Morreale, *Got Issues Much: Celebrities Share Their Traumas and Triumphs*, pp. 13-14, 17.

[234] Source: Bill Adler, *Jewish Wit and Wisdom*, p. 48.

[235] Source: Chuck Jones, *Chuck Redux: Drawing from the Fun Side of Life*, pp. 192-193.

[236] Source: Martha Sigall, *Living Life Inside the Lines: Tales from the Golden Age of Animation*, pp. 92-93.

[237] Source: Karen Adir, *The Great Clowns of American Television*, p. 74.

[238] Source: Ken Levine, "The kiss of death for Eddie LeBec." Blogspot. 21 July 2006 <http://tinyurl.com/kkvkhz4>.

[239] Source: John Anderson, "Robert Rodriguez unleashes edgy 'Machete.'" *Newsday*. 31 August 2010 <http://www.popmatters.com/pm/article/130405-robert-rodriguez-unleashes-edgy-machete/>.

[240] Source: Roger Ebert, "Virginia, Michael & Elaine Madsen: From Chicago to their dreams." *Chicago Sun-Times*. From June 13, 1986; revised 11/17/08. <http://rogerebert.suntimes.com/apps/pbcs.dll/article?AID=/19860613/PEOPLE/811189998/1023>.

[241] Source: Garrison Keillor, "O little town of Bethlehem, Pennsylvania." Tribune Media Services. 25 December 2007 <http://iht.com/articles/2007/12/25/opinion/edkeillor.php>.

[242] Source: Katie Forster, "Brian Blessed: 'The greatest danger in life is not taking the adventure.'" *Guardian*. 10 October <http://tinyurl.com/oxa9xcz>.

[243] Source: Kevyn Aucoin, Face*Forward*, p. 102.

[244] Source: Gary Younge, "Let me tell you a story." *The Guardian*. 23 January 2008 <http://www.guardian.co.uk/g2/story/0,,2245179,00.html>.

[245] Source: Emma Brockes, "Kristen Wiig: 'My next movie – it's going to be a Porky's prequel.'" *Guardian*. 18 November 2011 <http://www.guardian.co.uk/film/2011/nov/18/kristen-wiig-bridesmaids>.

[246] Source: Bob Madison, *American Horror Writers*, pp. 52,55.

[247] Source: Stephen Armstrong, "Wallace & Gromit are back on TV." *The Times*. 21 December 2008 <http://entertainment.timesonline.co.uk/tol/arts_and_entertainment/tv_and_radio/article5358866.ece>.

[248] Source: Jimmy Crum and Carole Gerber, *How About That!*, p. 10.

[249] Source: Don Knotts, *Barney Fife and Other Characters I Have Known*, pp. 67-68.

[250] Source: Anne Saidman, *Oprah Winfrey: Media Success Story*, pp. 17-18.

[251] Source: an American Masters public TV program featuring Jack Paar.